The Power of Picture Books

The Power of Picture Books

Using Content Area Literature in Middle School

Mary Jo Fresch
The Ohio State University at Marion

Peggy Harkins
The Ohio State University at Marion

National Council of Teachers of English
1111 W. Kenyon Road, Urbana, Illinois 61801-1096

Staff Editor: Carol Roehm-Stogsdill

Interior Design: Doug Burnett

Cover Design: Frank Cucciare

NCTE Stock Number: 36331

Library of Congress Cataloging-in-Publication Data

Fresch, Mary Jo, 1952–
    The power of picture books : using content area literature in middle school / Mary
Jo Fresch, Peggy Harkins.
        p. cm.
    Includes bibliographical references.
    ISBN 978-0-8141-3633-1 ((pbk))
  1. Content area reading—Study and teaching (Middle school) 2. Picture books—
Study and teaching (Middle school) I. Harkins, Peggy, 1948– II. Title.
    LB1050.455.F76 2009
    428.4071'2—dc22
                                                                                2009024613

To my husband, Hank; to my daughter, Angela, and her husband, Nate; and to my son, Mike, and his wife, Lori—for showing me the power of love. ~ MJF

To my husband, Rich; my son, Richard, and his wife, Tasha; my son, Ross, and his wife, Beth; and, most especially, to Solomon and Ethan, who will someday be middle school students in need of dedicated teachers. ~ PH

Contents

Permission Acknowledgments

Grateful acknowledgment is made to the following for permission to reprint copyrighted material:

A Crossing of Zebras: Animal Packs in Poetry by Marjorie Maddox, illustrated by Philip Huber (Wordsong, an imprint of Boyds Mills Press, 2008). Reprinted with permission of Boyds Mills Press, Inc.

Cover from *Into the Volcano* by Donna O'Meara is used with permission of Kids Can Press Ltd. Text © 2005 Donna O'Meara.

Cover from KAMISHIBAI MAN by Allen Say. Jacket art © 2005 by Allen Say. Reprinted by permission of Houghton Mifflin Harcourt Publishing Company. All rights reserved.

Cover from *One Well: The Story of Water on Earth* written by Rochelle Strauss, illustrated by Rosemary Woods is used with the permission of Kids Can Press Ltd. Text © 2007 Rochelle Strauss. Illustrations © Rosemary Woods.

Cover from TEAM MOON: How 400,000 People Landed Apollo 11 on the Moon by Catherine Thimmesh. Copyright © 2006 by Catherine Thimmesh. Reprinted by permission of Houghton Mifflin Harcourt Publishing Company. All rights reserved.

Cover from TWENTY-ONE ELEPHANTS AND STILL STANDING by April Jones Prince, illustrated by Francois Roca. Jacket art copyright © 2005 by Francois Roca. Reprinted by permission of Houghton Mifflin Harcourt Publishing Company. All rights reserved.

From CAVE DETECTIVES: UNRAVELING THE MYSTERY OF AN ICE AGE CAVE © 2007 by David L. Harrison and Ashley Mims. Used with permission of Chronicle Books, San Francisco. Visit ChronicleBooks.com.

From *Paper, Scissors, Sculpt!* © 2005 by Ben A. Gonzales. Used with permission from Sterling Publishing Co., Inc.

Illustration copyright © 2006 by R. Gregory Christie from DEAR MR. ROSEN-WALD by Carole Boston-Weatherford. Scholastic Inc./Scholastic Press. Reprinted by permission.

Louis Sockalexis: Native American Baseball Pioneer copyright © 2007 by Bill Wise. Illustrations copyright © 2007 by Bill Farnsworth. Permission arranged with Lee & Low Books, Inc., New York, NY 10016.

Acknowledgments

We'd like to thank the graduate students in our middle childhood Master of Education program for showing us the need for—and the value of—this book. A special thanks goes to Tasha Harkins for sharing her expertise in mathematics and to Richard Harkins for technical assistance.

1 The Power of Picture Books

The answers you get from literature depend on the questions you pose.
—Margaret Atwood

Consider the following passages from social studies, science, and mathematics:

> The warrior must stand in the middle of a meadow, up to his knees in rushes. Nine members of the Fianna will hurl their spears at him; he must defend himself with only a shield and hazel stick. If he is wounded, he has failed the test. (Harpur, 2007, unpaged)

> The ollie is a skateboard move for hopping over objects. . . . The science behind an ollie is about shifting your weight and obeying Newton's third law of motion ("For every action there is an equal and opposite reaction"). (Mercer, 2006, p. 13)

> A number's a number, right? Wrong, says Sam. We've got natural numbers (1, 2, 3, and so on) and whole numbers, which are the natural numbers and zero (0, 1, 2, 3 . . .)—hey, did you know that when Indian mathematicians first began using zero, the Europeans actually thought it was evil? (Lee & O'Reilly, 2007, p. 9)

Where might we find such rich descriptions? In a textbook? Indeed not. These passages come from "picture books" meant for older readers. These texts draw us in while simultaneously teaching something new and engaging about their topics. As textbooks expand upwards to 900 pages in length, few snag the interests of middle school students. More does not make better. Yet as educators, we realize the importance of content studies. Not only must we meet the goals of national or state content standards, but we also have the responsibility to develop informed citizens in a democratic society.

This book is a guide to literature that deepens the content we explore with middle school students. The National Council of Teachers of English (2004) suggests in *A Call to Action: What We Know about Adolescent Literacy and Ways to Support Teachers in Meeting Students' Needs* that adolescents need "sustained experiences with diverse texts in a variety of genres and offering multiple perspectives on real life experiences. Although many of these texts will be required by the curriculum, others should be self-selected and of high interest to the reader" (unpaged). The International Reading Association's Position Statement on Adolescent Literacy (Moore, Bean, Birdyshaw, & Rycik, 1999) suggests, "adolescents deserve access to a wide variety of reading material that they can and want to read" (p. 4) and "instruction that builds both the skill and desire to read increasingly complex materials" (p. 6). Desire to read and access to content are paramount in developing middle school students' knowledge about subject areas.

The picture book is an ideal genre for developing interest in reading and content. We define a picture book as one in which the text and illustrations have an important, supporting relationship. As Harris and Hodges (1995) explain, a picture book is "a book in which the illustrations are as important as the text" (p. 188). While picture books are often considered material for young readers, many illustrated texts are appropriate for older students in both content and visual composition. Bishop and Hickman (1992) suggest, "The standards for (picture) books particularly suited to older readers will differ from those for younger readers in degree rather than in kind. In general, they will vary along three dimensions: content, length or complexity, and sophistication" (p. 8). Therefore, we have included photo essays, illustrated texts, and many that display primary documents. Truly, many books that deal with middle school content happen to be picture books.

"But wait," you say. "This all sounds great, but I've already got a good textbook. Isn't that enough?"

Maybe not. Many teachers in the middle school do rely entirely on textbooks to familiarize students with content material. After all, students need a source for information about mathematics, science, social studies, the language arts, and the fine arts. But are textbooks really the best choice? Not entirely.

Limitations of Textbooks

Take a look at the average textbook. It is filled with charts, facts, photos, sidebars, suggested activities, and more—all competing with the content area material (Daniels & Zemelman, 2003/2004). All the extras may actually create confusion and distract students from the information they are meant to learn. In other words, textbooks sometimes fail in their mission to provide content in an understandable way.

Some textbooks read like an encyclopedia. So many details are included in an effort to be comprehensive that content may be treated superficially (Daniels & Zemelman, 2004; Zemelman, Daniels, & Hyde,

2005). In their 1998 study of textbooks, Chambliss and Calfee found this "skimpy treatment" (p. 7) in many books. They state, "a sixth-grade social studies book in our sample devotes one chapter to the continent of Africa and a short paragraph to North and South Korea" (p. 7). To no one's surprise, many students may find such textbook formats both confusing and boring. After all, when each paragraph is stuffed with facts, there's less room for the imaginative language that makes reading pleasurable (Chick, 2006; Sanacore, 1993).

Essentially textbooks are reference books, written by specialists with specialized vocabulary (Miller, in Olness, 2007). Not everyone takes pleasure in reading that kind of text. Yet our goal as teachers is to go beyond making students read, and to make them *want* to read (Johnson & Giorgis, 2001; Tunnell & Jacobs, 2008). Textbooks do have many strengths, but making students want to read is not typically one of them. Connecting to a student's prior knowledge and experiences is often a problem with textbooks, thus pushing the uninterested student farther away (Chambliss & Calfee, 1998).

Let's consider perspective. Can a textbook written in California, published in New York, and sold to schools across the United States really speak to the perspectives of local students? Obviously not. Life in California really *is* different from life in Nebraska or Rhode Island or Louisiana. So a passage that makes sense to a student from San Diego may seem silly or confusing to someone who lives in Omaha. Yet publishers frequently agree to some populous states' demands to include certain material. That's because whatever their selection committees choose must be used statewide (Hubisz, 2003). Relying on a single textbook for content also sends a message that it's okay to depend on one perspective (Daniels & Zemelman, 2003/2004), a view that is counterproductive to critical thinking.

Thoughtful cultural perspectives are sometimes absent from textbooks as well. According to Manning and Baruth (2004), some of the mistakes made by publishers include showing interaction of various groups only with European Americans; emphasizing male, middle-class, and mainstream European perspectives; highlighting historical concerns rather than current ones; and including only "safe" content. Because publishing companies have to survive in a competitive marketplace, they are likely to "delete whatever might offend anyone" (Ravitch, 2003, p. 78). Though this problem will not be evident in every textbook, teachers should consider whether the text they love is lacking in cultural inclusiveness.

A debate in the Sacramento schools demonstrates the problems some textbooks present regarding cultural sensitivity. A *San Francisco Chronicle* reporter (Burress, 2006) described a meeting of the California State Board of Education subcommittee that had to be cleared by security guards because of impassioned negative community reactions to a middle school social studies textbook. One student complained about the way her culture was represented. "'Learning about Hinduism in my sixth-grade class left me feeling ashamed and angry. . . . All that was talked about was the caste system, polytheism and sati.' (Sati is the long-banned burning of widows on a husband's funeral pyre.)" (Burress, 2006, second paragraph).

It is surprising to learn that some textbooks fail to provide consistently accurate and current information. Gone are the days (at least for the most part) when students would read a textbook that predicts a possible moon landing some time in our nation's future. But even when textbooks are new, the sheer volume of information created on a daily basis means "it is not humanly possible to keep current—or correct" (Raloff, in Daniels & Zemelman, 2003/2004, p. 39). A teacher using a textbook as the only basis for content must find other sources to check for accuracy (Daniels & Zemelman, 2004).

One of the most important considerations for teachers is whether textbooks match the reading abilities of students. Teachers know their students will be performing at widely different levels. Students with learning disabilities and those for whom English is a second (and maybe, emergent) language complicate things even more. Many content area textbooks are not easy to read (Sanacore, 1993; Zemelman, Daniels, & Hyde, 2005). Written to meet the needs of a "typical" student, they will not meet the reading needs of all students. It is unfortunate that some students will be unable to access the information contained in their texts (Moore, Bean, Birdyshaw, & Rycik, 1999, p. 4).

Though some textbooks try to provide reading hints, such as bold-face words followed by pronunciations, Chambliss and Calfee (1998) liken this to "reading an encyclopedia aloud" (p. 7). Instead, let's imagine students eager to dive into a book, share personal experiences that connect to content, while expanding their subject knowledge and vocabulary. Let's explore picture books as a perfect solution for adding depth and breadth to our curriculum.

Why Add Picture Books to Content Area Curricula?

So what *is* the solution to the difficulties textbooks present? Not every textbook is deficient and not in every area. However, including children's literature in the curriculum can mitigate the problems that do exist. While books of various genres are appropriate for supplementing textbooks, picture books have a number of advantages.

One feature that is unique about this genre is—the pictures! In a picture book, the illustrations complement and/or enhance the written word. They may provide a lot of informative detail not included in the text. In a sense, they "fill in the blanks" for the reader, establishing characterization, elaborating on the setting, and conveying moods and emotions (Sheridan, 2001). Because the pictures enhance the information in the text or expand the narrative in some way, students must use critical thinking to analyze what the illustrations do that the print does not. Often such analysis opens the door to discussion regarding interpretation. So the uniqueness of a picture book allows in-depth discussions that are often not possible with textbooks.

The illustrations in picture books also have value in and of themselves. They provoke an aesthetic response that draws on emotions and past experiences (Cox & Many, in Connor, 2003). The pictures, often exquisitely beautiful, are works of art. In fact, for many children it is the picture book that provides their introduction to the art world (Wolfenbarger & Sipe, 2007). So for many readers, the illustrations are a primary source of pleasure.

But picture books go beyond providing reading enjoyment. On a personal level, they also encourage the use of imagination, provide students with vicarious experiences, and help readers understand human behavior (Giorgis & Hartman, 2000). In doing so, picture books connect students to content on an affective level. Some topics cannot be easily separated from that emotional component. How can we consider slavery, for example, without also considering the emotional impact on the individuals involved? In exploring this kind of unit, teachers would want to touch not only students' minds but also their hearts. Picture books can do that.

It is easy to put too much emphasis on the visual elements in picture books. The text, however, is very important. In a picture book, the words and illustrations work together to communicate the message. It is from this unique combination of visual and verbal elements that students construct meaning (Pantaleo, 2007). Picture book texts offer the advantage of being short or organized into sections that are relatively brief, so students are not overwhelmed by the density of too much print on a page. Unconstrained by the need to fill each page with facts, picture book authors are free to use expressive language and rich imagery that both educate and enrich the reader. Picture book language can even serve as a model for their writing (Saunders, 1999).

Academically, picture book topics offer valuable extensions to subject area content and, in many cases, go far beyond the basic information in the textbook (Tunnell & Jacobs, 2008). For instance, Mr. Sirotto, an eighth-grade mathematics teacher, had been teaching probability for several weeks. When one student said, "Why do we have to learn this stuff?" Mr. Sirotto turned to a picture book to show real-life application. Imagine the surprise (yet intense interest) of the eighth graders when he began a Monday class by reading aloud *A Very Improbable Story* (Einhorn, 2008). After hearing the story, the students' assignment was to find personal experiences that paralleled what happened to the boy in the story. Reading the picture book aloud made the point to Mr. Sirotto's students that probability *is* an everyday topic and really piqued their interest in learning how to apply it to the real world. And Mr. Sirotto had the opportunity to see his students apply what they were learning in math.

Picture books generally focus on relatively narrow topics, so they are useful for introducing new concepts as well (Farris & Fuhler, 1994; Landt, 2007; Olness, 2007; Wysocki, 2004). Ms. Westwood, a sixth-grade language arts teacher, found that her district's curriculum materials skimmed over the teaching of idioms. She had a high English language learner population and felt she needed to introduce some new idioms that seemed to confuse the students. So she turned to *You Let the Cat Out of the Bag! (And Other Crazy Animal Sayings)* (Klingel, 2008) to get the conversation going. She discovered that this entertaining picture book provided the perfect platform for her students to open up about the phrases that perplexed them. The book helped the students make personal connections and provided a collective experience for the entire class (Landt, 2007).

The fact that picture books can provide alternative perspectives to those found in textbooks (Chick, 2006; Olness, 2007) cannot be overemphasized. When Mrs. Bentley, a seventh-grade science teacher, overheard her students discussing global warming, she decided she needed to go beyond what their textbook offered. While the *science* of global warming was apparent in the textbook, she wanted to tap into students' emotional sides. She selected *The Down-to-Earth Guide to Global Warming* (David & Gordon, 2007). With humor and text-friendly wording, the authors appealed to the middle schoolers and the topic took on a renewed focus in Mrs. Bentley's class.

As a textbook supplement, picture books also offer opportunities for greater inclusion of various cultures. Students need to "see themselves" represented in the materials used in classrooms, but textbooks rarely have the space to explore any culture in depth. Picture books can help fill that gap. This is doubly important for students who are learning English as a second language. One emphasis of an English as a Second Language (ESL) or an English Language Learning (ELL) program should be "integrating students' cultural experiences and background into meaningful language learning" (Manning & Baruth, 2004, p. 281). Picture books offer an ideal solution.

In addition to using culturally relevant texts, teachers of English language learners must also concentrate on building vocabulary. Hickman, Pollard-Durodola, and Vaughn (2004) recommend repeated readings of concise texts of 200 to 250 words, chosen to match students' interests. While teachers could divide novels into shorter passages, another approach might be to use picture books. Many are short enough to be read in one sitting, and the pictures can provide clues to word meanings. Those written for middle school students feature both familiar and challenging vocabulary that make the books appropriate for all students. With teacher read-alouds cited as "the most consistent activity used by classroom teachers . . . to enhance the literacy of ELLs by integrating effective vocabulary development practices" (Hickman, Pollard-Durodola, & Vaughn, 2004, p. 721), it makes sense for teachers to use picture books for that purpose.

Picture books may be used to let students pursue related interests that lie outside the content of their textbooks. This takes the middle school curriculum beyond the "tradition of simply accumulating and storing facts" (Beane, 1993, p. 32) by promoting deeper understanding. Because picture books are available on many levels of difficulty, this kind of meaningful personal research is not limited only to students who are already good readers. Less able readers can also participate along with their classmates (Freeman & Person, 1998). Even students with limited reading skills can take a meaningful role in classroom activities through the use of wordless picture books or those with little text (Sheridan, 2001).

Although a teacher's first concern is providing instruction, we must always remember that students have lives outside of the classroom. We are more than teachers of subject matter. We are also teachers of children and adolescents. As such, picture books are useful in addressing issues that may impact learning. Picture books may aid students in resolving conflicts by providing vicarious experiences and appropriate examples (Luke & Myers, 1995). They can also explore values that are largely unaddressed in many textbooks. For example, students can learn about moral courage by reading books about the Holocaust (Silverman, 2007). A relatively new problem addressed by picture books is to increase the coping skills of immigrant children whose lives are destabilized by the move to a new country (Baghban, 2007). Finally, picture books can be used to help students heal after experiencing some emotional trauma (Manifold, 2007), such as illness or a death in the family.

Maybe you're thinking, "Picture books sound great, and I'd really love to use them, but my students are too old for that genre." Costello and Kolodziej (2006) note that the idea that some students believe picture books are beneath them is rapidly diminishing. Indeed, the Caldecott Medal, awarded each year for outstanding children's book illustrations, "defines the picture book audience as birth to age 14" (Fingerson & Killeen, 2006, p. 32). Many topics tackled by picture book authors are more appropriate for middle school students and are created with the adolescent reader in mind. Their topics are sophisticated, inviting in-depth discussion. Issues that are important and very real to young adolescents—homelessness, crime, environmental problems (Beane, 1993)—are easily explored through picture books. The mature content of these books, written specifically for middle school readers, lends itself to opportunities for thoughtful analysis and critical thinking.

In addition, it makes no sense to downplay the importance of pictures when visual images abound in our society (Hibbing & Rankin-Erickson, 2003; Wolfenbarger & Sipe, 2007). Many students have learned to extract meaning from these visual images and rely on them to construct their understandings from text (Costello & Kolodziej, 2006). It's appropriate that they do so. After all, the arts of language are not limited to listening, speaking, reading, and writing. They also include viewing and visual representation (Lamping, Mack, & Johnson, 2007).

The way picture books are presented may also influence students' attitudes toward them. By emphasizing the rich vocabulary and high-level thought that goes into these books, teachers can show students that "the shorter text does not indicate easier material" (Costello & Kolodziej, 2006, p. 28). They can assure students that these are not just "baby" books. Seeing their teacher reading, enjoying, and discussing picture books with students and peers may also help convince them of the books' value.

"A picture book is a dialogue between two worlds: the world of images and the world of words" (Marcus, 2002, p. 3). Teachers of middle school students have the opportunity to open that dialogue with their students. By including picture books in the content areas, teachers add another dimension to literature. This added dimension could increase learning possibilities across the curriculum, not only for high achievers but also for all learners. Enjoyment, motivation, and real learning—they all flow from the power of the picture book.

Inviting All Learners—Differentiating Instruction through Picture Books

Educators have long abandoned the notion that a student's mind is a blank slate or, as the Romans put it, a "tabula rasa." Each learner possesses various qualities that influence his or her learning—prior experiences, learning styles, depth of vocabulary, home languages, home cultures, desire (or not) to read, and reading abilities. In the meantime, we have pressures to teach particular content in the constraints of one school year. Add the personal engagement issue to the mix and we often feel we are rolling a bowling ball down the middle of a football field hoping to bump one pin!

How can we account for these differing qualities and create instruction that engages all learners? Asking everyone to turn to page 486 in their textbook is most likely not going to work. Yes, it will "cover" the material, but we want more. We want all students to join the dialogue about a topic, to get excited about what they are learning, and to have memorable learning experiences.

While picture books could allow differentiated instruction in a number of ways, focusing on the five areas of the language arts provides a practical way to analyze how we could teach content to include all learners. The five areas are *speaking, listening, reading, writing,* and *viewing*.

Speaking is a good place to begin differentiation. Because both text and illustrations (or photographs) are equally important in picture books, conversations naturally follow. Small groups, buddies, or literature circles (Johnson & Freedman, 2005) that assign differing conversational roles to participants encourage dialogues about books and content. Students can verbalize connections to their personal life, thus giving the teacher a "window" to their home experiences. Students reveal their understanding when conversing with a peer or teacher. They must employ new vocabulary, synthesize ideas heard from the book or during the following conversations, and develop content-specific knowledge.

In the national standards set by learned societies (see Appendix A), students are expected to actively participate in inquiry, to be able to both discuss and explain their knowledge, and to adjust their use of language "to communicate effectively with a variety of audiences and for different purposes" (ReadWriteThink.org, #4). While this seems like a tall order, the carefully selected picture book invites and inspires such conversations.

Listening to picture books read aloud by teachers provides a basis for developing not only content knowledge but also literacy skills. Students hear vocabulary that may be beyond their reading levels but is important to the subjects they are learning. Hearing the nuances of the language spoken by a native speaker provides additional support and access for English language learners. Modeling provided by the teacher may draw in reluctant readers and engage them in the enjoyment literature can bring. Teachers can also bring topics to students that they might not otherwise choose to read about. Through listening we encourage conversations. It is a natural and powerful connection.

So how powerful can the connection between the read-aloud and the content be? Carlisle (1992) read aloud picture books about elderly people to her sixth graders. She selected varying viewpoints about aging and in particular found that the picture books "provided the economy necessary to convey this message to the students quickly and intelligently" (p. 52). After hearing all the books, the students "embarked on an impressive and highly sophisticated discussion" (p. 54). These picture books and topics, most likely overlooked by sixth graders, tied listening to speaking. As one of the students in Carlisle's class noted, "I can't believe this one beensy book kept us talking for about six days" (p. 57). Indeed, we believe picture books can provide engaging listening experiences.

Reading occurs across the curriculum, regardless of content area. *Adolescent Literacy: An NCTE Policy Research Brief* (2007) suggests, "reading materials should be appropriate and should speak to adolescents' diverse interests and varying abilities" (p. 4). As well, the goal of any teacher of adolescents is convincingly put forward in *Adolescent Literacy: A Position Statement* (Moore et al., 1999), "adolescents deserve teachers who understand the complexities of individual adolescent readers, respect their differences, and respond to their characteristics" (p. 8). By getting to know our students as learners, we can use picture books to differentiate instruction to meet their reading needs. Charts and tables that march across textbook pages often confuse struggling readers. As well, the layout of text can be difficult to follow. One look at the long list of professional materials explaining reading in the content fields gives us the notion that it's not that easy to do or teach (e.g., Brozo & Simpson, 2007; Fisher & Frey, 2008; Richardson, Morgan, & Fleener, 2006; Sadler, 2001; Vacca & Vacca, 2008).

Even the average reader needs support in textbooks often written above their reading level. Imagine the struggling reader's experience. Statistics from the National Assessment of Educational Progress show that "38 percent of U.S. students were found to have reading proficiency levels below 'basic.' Indeed, between 1992 and 2005 there was no significant change in the percentage of fourth graders reading at or above the 'basic' category in the United States" (Brozo & Flynt, 2007, p. 192).

While students may have fallen behind in their reading progress, not keeping pace with content learning has future repercussions. How can we be certain that students build knowledge if they cannot access the textbooks that teach it? Picture books open the door to using texts of varying levels. Focused on the same content, the picture books can provide additional support with engaging photographs or illustrations, humorous anecdotes, selective vocabulary, and high-interest content. We have the opportunity to nudge our reluctant and struggling readers toward picking up books and connecting with them.

Students who struggle with *writing* can find approachable models with picture books. In particular, English Language Learners will find repeated experiences with high-frequency sight words, support of illustrations, and scaffolding of new vocabulary (Reid, 2002). Struggling readers or students who lack prior knowledge of a topic may find picture books useful references as they write reports, journals, or their own books modeled after a picture book.

Students will find a starting place in forming opinions and personal stances about topics taught in a content area. For instance, a social studies teacher might use the picture book *Lady Liberty: A Biography* (Rappaport, 2008) to encourage research and writing about patriotic symbols in the United States. Further research about current day monuments could extend into writing proposals for a new memorial. Using the book as a starting point, students of various levels of writing skill can begin drafting their persuasive pieces. Such drafts provide insights into students' writing abilities and vocabulary. Many picture books provide the opportunity for models of group work, thus providing peer support in the writing process. The picture book provides the perfect example of employing interesting language to "capture" the reader.

Viewing engages readers in the images in the text. Hancock (2007) describes this aspect of language arts as "the observation and interpretation of a visual, nonprint form or format that results in personal meaning-making" (p. 7). We attend "to communication conveyed by . . . nonverbal visual means" (NCTE, 1996, p. 76). The power of viewing becomes apparent in a study of high school students' reading *The Middle Passage: White Ships/Black Cargo*. Connor (2003) found that this wordless picture book about slavery, "with its mature themes and powerful images . . . [leveled] . . . the playing field in most heterogeneous classrooms by creating new spaces and greater opportunities" (p. 244). Here, in the pictures, everyone is a reader of the visual representation of a powerful narrative.

Authors and illustrators of picture books have the opportunity to explore topics in greater depth than textbook writers possibly can. Such expansive presentations allow the author to *show* their topic—through illustrations and connected text. A student with little previous experience or knowledge about a topic can *see* content. We know the amount of visual media students meet today has greatly increased (Costello & Kolodziej, 2006). Allowing students to explore the visual elements of a picture book encourages speaking and writing. The "pictures" on the page "put more ideas in your head" (Hibbing & Rankin-Erikson, 2003, p. 758) and suddenly conversations about content take off.

And so we invite you to consider your learners, the content you teach, and the engagement you hope to see in your students. Listen, speak, read, write, and view . . . picture books invite us to do all five.

The Adolescent Learner

Students in middle school are different from those in the elementary grades. "Change" is a word that comes to mind when considering these students, and that change is often rapid, unexpected, and uneven. Students are developing physically and emotionally as well as cognitively. Attention to these changes must be reflected in the curriculum. "In middle level grades, more than any other, the emphasis needs to be on whom we teach rather than on what we teach" (Manning & Bucher, 2009, p. 29).

In any given classroom, a teacher may see great diversity among his or her students. Adolescents are beginning to think abstractly, so it's important for educators to provide challenging activities. Yet many of these students also benefit from hands-on work and active learning. Having a choice of assignments will appeal to these young learners. Working in small groups may also help to individualize instruction to meet their needs.

Cognitive development affects a student's social development and vice versa (Manning & Bucher, 2009). James Beane (1993) recommends an integrated curriculum that focuses on students' personal and social concerns. Personal concerns include things such as their search for identity or their desire to be independent. Global warming or human rights issues are among the social concerns middle school students may have. Beane further calls for a curriculum that emphasizes reflection, problem solving, ethical considerations, and building personal values.

Picture books are perfect for integrating the curriculum, and they can help teachers meet the needs of adolescents. They address a wide range of topics that appeal to the middle school learner. In addition, they can serve as a springboard for critical reading, writing, and discussion, as well as meaningful hands-on activities. By offering opportunities for group discussion and projects, they also fulfill students' social and emotional needs.

Take out a picture book. Read it aloud and enjoy it with your class. Let it provide the context for learning. Then, plan a follow-up lesson that encourages students to delve into the content in ways that appeal to them. You'll find there are many reasons why picture books belong in middle school.

How to Use This Book

This quick guide is organized with teachers of content areas in mind. Each chapter targets a particular area of the curriculum (social studies, mathematics, science, language arts, and the arts). Within each content area chapter we present featured picture books with related activities, cross-curricular connections, and a text set of related titles. Thus, content area teachers will find dozens of picture books that fit the middle school curriculum. So, how did we choose the featured books? We considered five important characteristics in selecting them:

- Relationship of the text with the accompanying illustrations or photographs
- Content that meets the requirements of middle school curriculum
- Sophistication of the subject matter
- Content that will engage students and teachers alike, and
- Complexity of language that respects the needs of middle school students.

Although some of the featured books have won (or may win) awards, that was not one of our selection criteria. Additionally, we limited our choices to books published in 2002 or later.

A synopsis of each book allows you to evaluate how it will fit in your planning. A number of activities to use with the book are presented. Each activity is coded to allow you to quickly assess the time needed to complete the task. One clock (☻) identifies an activity that could be completed in one class period. Two clocks (☻☻) indicate an activity that may be expanded into a more in-depth study and/or may require out of class work. These activities are not meant to be prescriptive, but rather starting points for ways to use each featured book. Suggested teaching strategies in the activities are explained in Appendix B, should you be unfamiliar with them. Only you know your setting and population, special interests of students, curriculum, and team of teachers. We hope you will consider the activities for each of these featured books as a launching pad for your own creative ideas.

Cross-curricular connections facilitate the use of the book for interdisciplinary planning. Middle school teams will find this particularly helpful as these connections provide continued use of the books across the curriculum. Check the listing at the end of each chapter for all the books in other content areas that have a cross-curricular use. This allows a team of middle school teachers easy ways to find the interdisciplinary uses of all the books in a particular content area. Of course, these are only suggestions. Our experiences tell us that talented content teachers find multiple ways to use literature.

A final feature for each book is a text set, a "collection of books related to a common element or topic" (Opitz, in Camp, 2000, p. 400). Think back to Mr. Sirotto's eighth-grade probability lesson with its text set to expand their studies or Mrs. Westwood's sixth-grade language arts lesson on idioms that opened the conversation about English. As Kettel and Douglas (2003) argue, text sets with a single theme encouraged the sixth graders they worked with to have "more engagement and, consequently, more comprehension" (p. 43). They suggest beginning by introducing a picture book, followed by a focused, related set of books that helps diversify reading levels and meets the interests of adolescents.

The books that complement the featured book are presented in a text set that has four criteria: (1) integration of additional genres, (2) wider range of reading difficulty to allow for differentiated instruction, (3) expansion of student interest in the topic, and (4) use of "tried and true" titles that may already be in your school or classroom library. We identify the genre of each book in the text sets by using the following "key":

- ABC = book organized around the alphabet
- AN = anthology
- B = biography
- FPB = fiction picture book
- FT = folktale
- FYA = fiction young adult
- NF = nonfiction
- P = poetry
- PB = picture book

Now you are armed with titles, ideas, and various Web supports . . . so what *do* you do with a picture book when you stand in front of a room full of middle school students? The books selected here can be read in snippets to motivate and entice, or in their entirety to create a common text for discussion and subsequent reading of related books. Ivey (2003) suggests "it is your knowledge about the world and your experiences that enable you to bring life to text—a voice to a text—that many students cannot yet achieve" (p. 813). In fact, we can think of no better "expert" to read aloud a content area picture book than a content area teacher. The read aloud provides the opportunity for you to share your passion about your subject in very unique ways. We have seen science teachers change voice, move about the room, even get into the "character" of a famous scientist as they read aloud to middle school students. We suggest you let your love for social studies, mathematics, science, language arts, or the arts guide your narration. We do think a little practice beforehand goes a long way to feeling comfortable . . . so give it a try. What better way to engage students in your subject?

"Within the pages of a picture book is the potential to entice, intrigue, and motivate . . . middle school readers as they vicariously experience times and places that make up their past, influence the present, and may have an impact upon their futures" (Farris & Fuhler, 1994, p. 47). What textbook can offer the same promise? Including picture books in the curriculum makes sense.

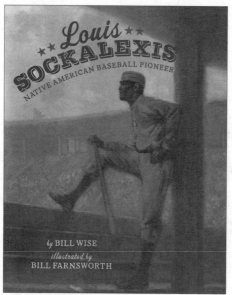

A.

B.

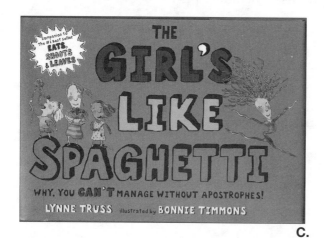

C.

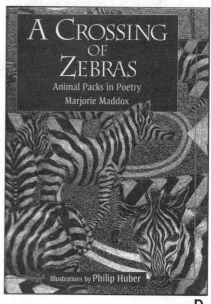

D.

A. *Louis Sockalexis: Native American Baseball Pioneer* by Bill Wise; illustrated by Bill Farnsworth. **B.** *My Librarian Is a Camel: How Books Are Brought to Children around the World* by Margriet Ruurs. **C.** *The Girl's Like Spaghetti: Why, You Can't Manage without Apostrophes* by Lynne Truss; illustrated by Bonnie Timmons. **D.** *A Crossing of Zebras: Animal Packs in Poetry* by Marjorie Maddox; illustrated by Phillip Huber.

2 Picture Book Invitations in Language Arts

The man who does not read books has no advantage over the man who cannot read them.

—Mark Twain

The language arts encompass all our literacy and literary skills. We read, write, speak, and listen every day. A quick glance through any state's standards makes us aware of the breadth of skills students must develop to be effective communicators. Whether it is listening, reading, writing, spelling, speaking, or viewing, students need multiple exposures to develop skills in the language arts. However, we also know skimming the surface of all these areas is not going to develop proficiency or independence. Rather, we must look to developing depth of knowledge. Filling out worksheets, memorizing lists of words, and reading the same "canon" of books each year is bound to bore students and teachers alike.

Need to work on vocabulary development? *You Let the Cat Out of the Bag (And Other Crazy Animal Sayings)* (Klingel, 2008) and *A Crossing of Zebras: Animal Packs in Poetry* (Maddox, 2008) are sure to make the English language interesting and understandable, especially to English Language Learners. Tired of sentences without punctuation? Spend a little time with *The Girl's Like Spaghetti: Why, You Can't Manage without Apostrophes!* (Truss, 2007) and your "red pen days" are over. After the students have fun with punctuation, jazz up their writing with *How to Write Stories: Pin Your Ideas to the Page!* (Warren, 2007).

Perspective is a key element in the authors' work. *Sugar Cane: A Caribbean Rapunzel* (Storace, 2007) and *The Titanic: An Interactive History Adventure* (Temple, 2008) show that men, women, children, class, and culture are all perspectives for students to consider when hearing or reading books. Of course, biographies can go anywhere in the curriculum . . . but the ones in this chapter provide multiple opportunities to discuss the important life work of many men and women. *Lucy Maud Montgomery: The Author of* Anne of Green Gables (Wallner, 2006) and *Louis Sockalexis: Native American Baseball Pioneer* (Wise, 2007), along with each text set, show that determination can cross gender, race, and socioeconomic status.

Students may never look at everyday items around them in the same way once you explore *One Million Things: A Visual Encyclopedia*

(Bryan, 2008). As well, they may never look at going to the library the same way once they view *My Librarian Is a Camel: How Books Are Brought to Children around the World* (Ruurs, 2005). Both books show just how important the pictures, illustrations, or photographs are to picture books in the middle grades.

The language arts are at the "heart" of our curriculum. (See Appendix A for national language arts standards.) It is the reading and writing we do every day that expresses who we are, teaches us about those around us, and communicates our ideas and feelings. Giving students personal experiences that make them "want to" read and write will set them on a path of lifelong literacy. And who knew it could be so much fun along the way?

Women Only—Biographies of Visionaries

Wallner, Alexandra. (2006). *Lucy Maud Montgomery: The Author of* Anne of Green Gables. New York: Holiday House. (B/PB)

Lucy Maud Montgomery (Maud) was born in Clifton, Prince Edward Island. Her mother died when Maud was 21-months-old, and her father left her in the strict care of her grandparents as he searched for a better life in Western Canada. Maud loved to read and write, keeping a journal to record what she saw, heard, and did while living so close to the ocean. She often sent her stories and poems to newspapers and magazines, hoping to have one published. At the age of 16, her first poem, *On Cape Leforce*, was printed in a Charlottetown newspaper. While studying to be a teacher, Maud continued to write. Using an idea from one of her journals, Maud wrote *Anne of Green Gables*. Her trials and tribulations as an author are carefully recounted in this biography. Insights into the woman who touched so many lives with her books will inspire any young writer.

Activity Suggestions

1. ☺ or ☺☺ *Dear diary:* Maud was a diligent journal writer. From this journal she drew ideas for poems and stories. Her idea for *Anne of Green Gables* came from a note she wrote: "Elderly couple apply to [orphanage] for a boy. By mistake a girl is sent to them." Students develop a story using their own journals or headlines from the newspaper.

2. ☺☺ *Maud's book club:* Create groups to discuss books. This could be done three different ways: (a) have all students read the same book and create a literature circle (see Appendix B) to discuss that book; (b) have students select different "Anne" books and gather to discuss plot, setting,

and characters; or (c) have students select a biography from the text set and later meet to discuss their book.

3. ☺☺ *Poetic license:* Maud fought the publisher of *Anne of Green Gables* for proper payment of royalties. She felt, as a woman, that they had cheated her. Many years later she won. Have students investigate how the publishing world accepts manuscripts for consideration (publishers' websites provide information for submitting manuscripts). Together, create a flowchart that describes the creative process from draft to submittal. There are several publishers who accept work by students (*Streetside* stories, *Highlights for Children*). Some students may choose to submit their work.

4. ☺☺ *No, no, no, no, no, FINALLY!* Maud sent publishers her original version of *Anne of Green Gables* five times only to have it rejected. Two years later, after carefully rewriting it, L. C. Page Company of Boston published the story. Have students research other authors to discover their challenges to being published. For instance, Kenneth Grahame, author of *Wind in the Willows*, was told his book was "an irresponsible holiday story," and *The Diary of Anne Frank* was reviewed as, "The girl doesn't, it seems to me, have a special perception or feeling which would lift that book above the 'curiosity' level" (http://www.writersservices. com/mag/m_rejection.htm). Many authors' biographies and autobiographies tell these stories, so allow students to select and read about their favorite author.

Cross-Curricular Connections

1. ☺ *Social studies:* At the back of the book, Wallner provides a list of books written by Maud. She notes that Maud did not write the "Anne" stories in chronological order and provides numbers next to the titles in the order they should have been written. Have students select any of the titles to read. Small groups can share the events of their books and create a timeline of the "Anne" book events.

2. ☺ *Mathematics:* The book tells of Maud taking notes after seeing the clipper ship *Marco Polo* that crashed in 1883 on Prince Edward Island during a storm. Where was it headed? Calculate the distance it traveled: how far it did go and how far it should have gone. The *Marco Polo* sailed for thirty-two years. Have students calculate the distances of each route taken (information is available on the Internet).

3. ☺☺ *Science:* Investigate famous women scientists. Students can use the Internet or biographies and autobiographies published about women who have made important scientific discoveries. They can share their

findings in a number of ways, such as perform mock interviews or role-play a speech by one of these women.

Suggested Text Set for Further Invitations

Colman, Penny. (2006). *Adventurous Women: Eight True Stories about Women Who Made a Difference*. New York: Henry Holt. (B)

Dray, Philip, and Stephen Alcorn. (2007). *Yours for Justice, Ida B. Wells: The Daring Life of a Crusading Journalist*. Illustrated by Stephen Alcorn. Atlanta, GA: Peachtree Publishers. (PB/B)

Giovanni, Nikki, and Bryan Collier. (2006). *Rosa*. Illustrated by Bryan Collier. New York: Scholastic. (B)

Harness, Cheryl. (2001). *Remember the Ladies: 100 Great American Women*. New York: HarperCollins. (B)

Hopkinson, Deborah, and Terry Widener. (2006). *Girl Wonder: A Baseball Story in Nine Innings*. Pictures by Terry Widener. New York: Aladdin Paperbacks. (FPB—based on the true story of Alta Weiss—an Ohio teen who played with an all-male semipro team in 1907.)

Kann, Bob. (2007). *A Recipe for Success: Lizzie Kander and Her Cookbook*. Madison, WI: Wisconsin Historical Society Press. (B)

Lewis, J. Patrick, and Mark Summers. (2005). *Vherses: A Celebration of Outstanding Women*. Illustrated by Mark Summers. Mankato, MN: Creative Editions. (P)

Steele, Philip. (2006). *Marie Curie: The Woman Who Changed the Course of Science*. Washington, DC: National Geographic. (B)

 ## Men Only—Biographies of Racial Tensions

Wise, Bill, and Bill Farnsworth. (2007). *Louis Sockalexis: Native American Baseball Pioneer*. Illustrated by Bill Farnsworth. New York: Lee & Low Books. (B/PB)

In 1884, twelve-year-old Louis Sockalexis, a Penobscot Indian, "fell in love with baseball" (unpaged). Living on a reservation in Maine, Louis learned the game when local boys playing on the other side of the river called for him to join them. Louis soon discovered that prejudice would find its way to the baseball diamond. Jeered while playing at a Catholic high school and Holy Cross College in Massachusetts, Louis struggled to keep his dream alive. Offered a contract to play with the Cleveland Spiders, Louis had to choose between his love of the game and his responsibilities to the reservation. Louis went on to play for Cleveland in 1897. At his first major league game, his father, along with members of his tribe, saw him hit a home run that would not only make baseball history but also quiet the boos and insults he had long endured.

Activity Suggestions

1. ☺☺ *The struggles of many:* Using the suggested text set and other available resources, have students investigate other biographies of people who have combated racism. Create a chart showing the name, their "claim to fame," culture, time period, challenges faced, and how they rose above the prejudice to accomplish their goals.

2. ☺ *Compare the versions:* Many other books about Louis Sockalexis exist. Have students create a matrix (see Appendix B) to record dates and details from each version. What details did each author choose to omit or include? Discuss what such an exercise tells us about writers of biography.

3. ☺ *What's in a name?* Origins of names, places, and Native American tribes can provide fascinating information for students. For instance, "Penobsoct" means "the place where the rocks open out." Use places mentioned in the book (e.g., Maine, Massachusetts, Cleveland) to discover word origins. Add local places or Native American tribes to extend the investigation of word histories.

4. ☺☺ *Analyzing sport team names:* On the last page of the book, the author notes explain that the Cleveland Spiders were renamed the Indians in 1915. Some say it was to honor Sockalexis. Others say it is derogatory. Other team names have been criticized as being offensive. Have students research the debates that have taken place surrounding these names. Suggest they offer new team names based on research about the team's location or most influential player.

Cross-Curricular Connections

1. ☺ *Social studies:* Map where Louis grew up, locating the Penobscot reservation mentioned in the book. Locate Holy Cross College in Massachusetts and Cleveland, Ohio. Follow the train lines from Penobscot, Holy Cross, and Cleveland to map his route from childhood to baseball fame.
2. ☺ *Mathematics:* Batting averages are used to evaluate the skill of a player. Louis's changing percentages (.400, .338) demonstrate this statistic. Have students compare the changes. How is this batting average calculated? Compare other current day players to Louis's averages.
3. ☺☺ *The arts:* Textiles used to create baseball uniforms have changed significantly over the years. Using the Baseball Hall of Fame website (http://exhibits.baseballhalloffame.org/dressed_to_the_nines/index.htm) or print resources, compare the differences in fabric. Follow one team's uniform over time and note the changes in not only fabric but also in color and design.

Suggested Text Set for Further Invitations

Bruchac, Joseph, and S. D. Nelson. (2004). *Jim Thorpe's Bright Path*. Illustrated by S. D. Nelson. New York: Lee & Low Books. (B)

Crowe, Ellie, and Richard Waldrep. (2007). *Surfer of the Century: The Life of Duke Kahanamoku*. Illustrated by Richard Waldrep. New York: Lee & Low Books. (B)

Haskins, James, Kathleen Benson, and Benny Andrews. (2006). *John Lewis in the Lead: A Story of the Civil Rights Movement*. Illustrated by Benny Andrews. New York: Lee & Low Books. (B)

Nelson, S. D. (2006). *Quiet Hero: The Ira Hayes Story*. New York: Lee & Low Books. (B)

Robinson, Sharon. (2004). *Promises to Keep: How Jackie Robinson Changed America*. New York: Scholastic Press. (B)

Taylor, Gaylia, and Frank Morrison. (2006). *George Crum and the Saratoga Chip*. Illustrated by Frank Morrison. New York: Lee & Low Books. (B)

Yoo, Paula, and Dom Lee. (2005). *Sixteen Years in Sixteen Seconds: The Sammy Lee Story*. Illustrated by Dom Lee. New York: Lee & Low Books. (B)

 ## Write On!

Warren, Celia. (2007). *How to Write Stories: Pin Your Ideas to the Page!* Laguna Hills, CA: QEB Publishing. (NF/PB)

Students are sure to draw a wealth of ideas from this brightly illustrated and visually interesting book about writing. Warren carefully guides students through the specifics of genre, creating character and setting, breaking writer's block, story mapping, and more. Each two-page spread has simulated "sticky notes" full of ideas, terms and definitions, and challenges for students. Entertaining stories expand the ideas and place descriptions in books that many students will already know. Warren provides tips, springboards, and suggested activities throughout this book that are sure to attract the most reluctant writer.

Activity Suggestions

1. ☺☺ *Which genre am I?* On pages 4 and 5, Warren explains the difference between various genres. Have small groups of students divide up and use the examples she provides to create a list of features that fit the genre. For instance, she mentions Karen Hesse's *Out of the Dust* as historical. Besides being "set in the past" (p. 4), what other features designate this book as "historical"? Have them suggest other books they have read that could be added to the list. Post these as ideas for independent reading throughout the year.

2. ☻ *A character by any other name:* Warren tells us (p. 4) that the name "Wendy" did not appear until J. M. Barrie used it to name the main character in *Peter Pan*. Later, she discusses "what's in a name" (p. 13) to show how name origins can be reflective of the character. (Did you know Tuck's name from *Tuck Everlasting* was chosen by Natalie Babbitt because it means "life?") E. B. White used meaningful names as well. (Have students look up "arable," the family name for the farmers in *Charlotte's Web*.) Using a baby name book (or the website www.behindthename.com), have students specifically select names for a character they want to write about. Have them share how the name they selected is reflective of that person's role in the story.

3. ☻☻ *A better word:* Students often get "stuck" using the same word over and over (such as "said"). Create classroom charts that students continually add to when they come across synonymous words. Have them propose words that seem to be most redundant in their writing and develop a personal list of alternatives.

4. ☻☻ *And you are selling that because . . . :* Bring in classified ads from the local newspaper. Allow students to select an ad and create a story behind the reason the item is being sold. Ask them to write it first as a nonfiction version and then again as a fantasy version. Compare the results by sharing aloud.

Cross-Curricular Connections

1. ☻☻ *Social studies:* Research the differences in alphabets. Have small groups find library resources (don't forget the encyclopedia!) to answer these questions and then share their findings: (a) what is the history of the alphabet we use? (b) what other alphabets do they know or have seen? (c) what of the historic nature of hieroglyphics do they know?

2. ☻ *Science:* Some studies have shown that drawing with the opposite hand you write with can "release" creativity. Have students give this a try. How many students are left-handed or right-handed? Chart the findings. If there's time, have students explore the definitions of "right-brained" and "left-brained." What do these mean in terms of their dominant hand?

3. ☻☻ *The arts:* Have students create their own "inspirations" for writing (photographs or paintings they find or create). Or, have students illustrate their own writings done in language arts. These could take the form of picture books that can be shared with younger readers.

Suggested Text Set for Further Invitations

Hest, Amy, and Sonja Lamut. (2005). *The Private Notebooks of Katie Roberts, Age 11*. Illustrated by Sonja Lamut. Cambridge, MA: Candlewick Press. (FYA)

Kinney, Jeff. (2007). *Diary of a Wimpy Kid*. New York: Amulet Books for Young People. (FYA)

McKissack, Pat, and Gordon C. James. (2007). *A Song for Harlem*. Illustrated by Gordon C. James. New York: Viking. (FYA)

Rumford, James. (2004). *Sequoyah: The Cherokee Man Who Gave His People Writing*. Boston: Houghton Mifflin. (B)

Shulevitz, Uri. (2005). *The Travels of Benjamin of Tudela: Through Three Continents in the Twelfth Century*. New York: Farrar, Straus, and Giroux.

 Getting to the Point with Punctuation!

Truss, Lynne, and Bonnie Timmons. (2007). *The Girl's Like Spaghetti: Why, You Can't Manage without Apostrophes!* Illustrated by Bonnie Timmons. New York: G. P. Putnam's Sons. (NF/PB)

Lynne Truss provides a fun romp through punctuation in this book. Author of the adult book and illustrated juvenile version *Eats, Shoots and Leaves,* Truss focuses on apostrophes. Timmons's illustrations help make the point of how "The dogs like my dad" is very different than "The dog's like my dad" (unpaged). At first glance this book seems fairly simple, but the complex nature of the correct use of apostrophes needs the analysis and discussion generated by the illustration. It is a great way to have students develop a deeper, conceptual knowledge of punctuation through Truss' (or is that Truss's?) paired sentences and Timmons's cartoon-like illustrations. Students (and you) are bound to laugh out loud. A two-page spread at the end of the book explains the differences between each pair (and uses the technical language "independent clause," "introductory clause," "coordinating adjectives," and so on).

Activity Suggestions

1. ☻ *Modeled after the book:* Have students create their own sentence pairs that change meaning when the apostrophe is used or not. Make the point that the apostrophe shows ownership (my brother's); not using it shows plurality (my brothers). Display the students' work and have them vote for their favorite pair.

2. ☻ *And now the comma*! Use Truss's other juvenile book (see text set) to explore the use of commas and how their use can change meaning

(you could use the classic "woman, without her, man is nothing" versus "woman without her man, is nothing". . . or save that for the teacher's lounge). Provide several sentences from the book and ask students how the insertion of a comma changes the meaning.

3. ☯ *What sort of apostrophe?* This book shows the apostrophe as a way to show possession or as a part of a contraction. Have students categorize each use throughout the book. Additionally, some of the possessive apostrophes are singular, while others are plural. Discuss the differences.

4. ☯ *Real world apostrophes:* Using the newspaper, have students highlight sentences that contain apostrophes. Classify them as contractions or possessives. See if rewriting the sentence without the apostrophe creates a different version, similar to those provided throughout the book by Truss. For instance, if a local paper had an article headlined as "Boy's in Trouble," this could be rewritten as "Boys in Trouble." How would that change the illustration?

Cross-Curricular Connections

1. ☯☯ *Social studies:* Examine the history of punctuation. The book by Don Robb provided in the text set gives sidebar information about the development of punctuation. Have students map the areas of the world (mentioned in the book) where early versions of our alphabet existed: proto-Sinaitic, Phoenicians, Greek, and Romans. How did invading peoples influence punctuation?

2. ☯ *Mathematics:* Commas are important in mathematics. They provide help in writing large numbers. How did the comma first come to be used for number notation? Use Ann McCallum's book from the set below, or other resources you have, to explore the history of mathematics in relation to the comma and the decimal (period).

3. ☯☯ *The arts*: Using the sentences created in language arts, have students illustrate their pair, showing how the apostrophe impacts their illustrations. Have them use any medium you prefer, or have them replicate Timmons's watercolor illustrations.

Suggested Text Set for Further Invitations

Carr, Jan, and Ethan Long. (2007). *Greedy Apostrophe: A Cautionary Tale*. Illustrated by Ethan Long. New York: Holiday House. (PB)

Donohue, Moira Rose, and Jenny Law. (2008). *Penny and the Punctuation Bee*. Illustrated by Jenny Law. Morton Grove, IL: Albert Whitman & Co. (PB)

McCallum, Ann, and Carolyn Norton. (2005). *The Secret Life of Math: Discover How (and Why) Numbers Have Survived from the Cave Dwellers to Us!* Illustrated by Carolyn Norton. Nashville, TN: Williamson Books. (NF)

Petty, Kate, and Jennie Maizels. (2006). *The Perfect Pop-Up Punctuation Book.* New York: Dutton Children's Books. (NF)

Pulver, Robin, and Lynn Rowe Reed. (2003). *Punctuation Takes a Vacation.* Illustrated by Lynn Rowe Reed. New York: Holiday House. (PB)

Robb, Don, and Anne Smith. (2007). *Ox, House, Stick: The History of Our Alphabet.* Illustrated by Anne Smith. Watertown, MA: Charlesbridge. (NF)

Truss, Lynne, and Bonnie Timmons. (2006). *Eats, Shoots & Leaves: Why, Commas Really Do Make a Difference!* Illustrated by Bonnie Timmons. New York: G. P. Putnam's Sons. (NF)

You Don't Say! Interpreting Idioms

Klingel, Cynthia Fitterer. (2008). *You Let the Cat Out of the Bag! (And Other Crazy Animal Sayings).* Illustrated by Mernie Gallagher-Cole. Mankato, MN: Child's World. (NF/PB)

Learning these idioms definitely will not "go in one ear and out the other." Gallagher-Cole's entertaining but "explaining" illustrations add to the fun of this book. Thirty-one common idioms are used in context, defined, and illustrated in a humorous way. "Take the bull by the horns" and get students to "go the extra mile" to talk about where they might have heard some of these idioms. Of course, the ones presented here are just "a drop in the bucket," but you will "hit the nail on the head" as you expand this aspect of language study. It can be "a shot in the arm" for your language arts instruction.

Activity Suggestions

1. ☺☺ *Chew the fat:* There are many more idioms to discuss. Have students interview family members for ones they use regularly and share these with the class. Ask them to write a context that uses the idiom (as in the book) and then to provide its meaning. (By the way, "chew the fat" came from the high seas. When sailors ran low on supplies, they would chew the layer of fat from salt pork. They often sat about, "chewing" and talking.) Create a class collection of these idioms.

2. ☺ *It's history now:* Many resources exist that provide the origins of idioms (see text set or go to http://www.phrases.org.uk/meanings/index.html). Have students choose an idiom and research its origin. For example, one idiom in the book is "once in a blue moon." According to

the website previously mentioned, "a blue moon refers to the second full moon that occurs in any calendar month. On average, there will be forty-one months that have two full moons in every century. By that calculation 'once in a blue moon' means once every two-and-a-half years." Have students use large paper to write the idiom, provide the meaning, and describe the origin. Post these to share.

3. ☺ or ☺☺ *It's just a charade*: Using the idioms in the book, have students silently act out the words, incorporating the literal illustrations provided. So, "a drop in the bucket" would be acted out to show something dropping into a bucket, or the idiom "egg on your face" might be acted out by the student "cracking" an egg and showing something dripping down their face. Once they act out the book idioms, ask them to expand to the ones they found on their own.

4. ☺☺ *Pop culture idioms:* Students can see that idioms are not just from "the olden days" but continue to develop in our language. Have them suggest phrases they say to their friends that have an idiomatic meaning (one that adults might need translated). For instance, you might use and explain phrases such as "we're not in Kansas anymore" (*Wizard of Oz*), "I'll be back" (*Terminator*), "life is a like a box of chocolates (*Forrest Gump*), and "down the rabbit hole" (*Alice in Wonderland*) as examples drawn from literature and movies that develop into common usage. Have them collect these over several days and then create a guide for listeners. This will be particularly helpful to English Language Learners.

Cross-Curricular Connections

1. ☺☺ *Social studies:* The time period around the Civil War provided many idioms that we still use today. Have students discuss the meaning of and research the origins of these (see website provided later) to get started: *your name is mud, bite off more than you can chew, cross your fingers, flash in the pan, go AWOL, in the nick of time,* and *chip on your shoulder.*

2. ☺☺ *Mathematics:* Many idioms are number-related. Have students brainstorm as many as possible. Then, discuss the math connection to the idiom. Have students create a class book of math idioms (maybe named "Idioms 'by the number'"). Use these to get started: *all sixes, back to square one, double take, feel like a million bucks, hindsight is twenty-twenty, I've got your number, one fell swoop, put two and two together, take forty winks, third degree,* and *whole nine yards.* (More available at http://www.usingenglish.com/reference/idioms/cat/34.html.)

3. 😊😊 *The arts:* This book is a perfect model for creating other "literal" translations of idioms. Have students illustrate an idiom found in their language arts class (such as "raining cats and dogs") that is similar to those done by Gallagher-Cole (black ink and watercolors), or use another medium being used in your current instruction. Great examples of literal illustrations are provided at the child-friendly "Eye on idioms" (http://www.readwritethink.org/materials/idioms/).

Suggested Text Set for Further Invitations

Arnold, Tedd. (2004). *Even More Parts: Idioms from Head to Toe*. New York: Dial Books for Young Readers. (PB)

Brennan-Nelson, Denise, and Jane Monroe Donovan. (2007). *My Grandma Likes to Say*. Illustrated by Jane Monroe Donovan. Chelsea, MI: Sleeping Bear Press. (PB)

Frasier, Debra. (2000). *Miss Alaineus: A Vocabulary Disaster*. San Diego: Harcourt Brace. (PB).

Klingel, Cynthia Fitterer. (2008). *Go Fly a Kite! (And Other Sayings We Don't Really Mean)*. Illustrated by Mernie Gallagher-Cole. Mankato, MN: Child's World. (NF)

Klingel, Cynthia Fitterer. (2008). *You're Clean as a Whistle! (And Other Silly Sayings)*. Illustrated by Mernie Gallagher-Cole. Mankato, MN: Child's World. (NF)

Tabor, Nancy. (2000). *Ve Lo Que Dices: Modismos en Español e Inglés (See What You Say: Spanish and English Idioms)*. Watertown, MA: Charlesbridge. (NF)

Terban, Marvin. (2006). *Scholastic Dictionary of Idioms*. New York: Scholastic. (NF)

 ## A Babble of Words

Maddox, Marjorie, and Philip Huber. (2008). *A Crossing of Zebras: Animal Packs in Poetry*. Illustrated by Philip Huber. Honesdale, PA: Wordsong. (P/PB)

An army of ants, a pride of lions, a school of fish . . . we all know about collective nouns. Maddox takes these descriptive phrases and crafts them into sophisticated and entertaining poetry. She also introduces some lesser-known ones—a rumba of rattlesnakes, a scurry of squirrels, and a crossing of zebras. Huber's scratchboard with color ink illustrations is fascinating to study and expand the poems . . . the army of ants are outfitted in military gear and carry an anti-anteater flag, the crash of rhinos collide at the park, and the leap of leopards "somersault toward the moon" (p. 17). Students will enjoy the complex illustrations that seem to allow us to peek into the secret lives of animals.

Activity Suggestions

1. ☺☺ *More please!* Maddox creates poems about fourteen different collective nouns. Have students research additional ones and create their own poems. These can be found on the web (http://www.askoxford.com/asktheexperts/collective/?view=uk) or in the books provided in the text set.

2. ☺ *What's your form?* Maddox uses a number of poetic "forms" to create her poems. For instance, the giraffe poem is concrete—tall and narrow—and the leopards' poem takes on the shape of them leaping. Give each student one poem to identify. How does the form enhance the meaning? What shape could they use for the poem writing in activity 1?

3. ☺ *Fools, jewels, ghouls—patterns in our language*: Poetry is the perfect place to analyze rhyme in English. Maddox often uses words that rhyme but have different spelling patterns (scare, bear, fair). Using three columns, have students write the rhymed words, separating the different spellings into different columns. Then, have them suggest other words that would fit in each of the columns (for instance, rare, stare, share, tear, wear, hair, flair).

4. ☺ *Perfect punctuation*: Analyze Maddox's use of punctuation to make the reader pause, read quickly, read slowly, and so on. Using other poems, compare how the author guides us to interpret the poetry as she or he hoped we would. How do students use punctuation in their poems to achieve this rhythm?

Cross-Curricular Connections

1. ☺☺ *Social studies:* In the author's notes, Maddox shares the origin of "school of fish." Originally, the word was *shoal*, meaning a large group. But handwritten manuscripts often had mistakes in them . . . and sometimes those mistakes stuck. Once the printing press was used regularly, our spellings became conventional and any handwritten errors remained. Have students examine the history of the printing press that William Caxton brought to England in 1476. What effect did this have on the common man? Are there other inventions at the same time that changed the lives of people?

2. ☺☺ *Science:* We can see the relationship between "a tower of giraffes" and the actual animal. Have students research animal behavior (a scurry of squirrels) that influenced the collective noun used to describe them. Why do we say "a pride of lions" or "a murder of crows?"

3. ☻☻ *The arts:* On page 22 is the poem "A band of coyotes." The illustration is a band, with coyotes as the musicians, performing on a stage in front of the animal kingdom. Maddox uses two colors of print to show multiple voices in the poem. Have the students interpret and perform the poem as music. Or have the students illustrate the poems they wrote in language arts (see *More please!*) using Huber's scratchboard method.

Suggested Text Set for Further Invitations

Ayto, John. (1991). *Dictionary of Word Origins*. New York: Arcade. (NF)

Browne, Philippa-Alys. (1996). *A Gaggle of Geese: The Collective Names of the Animal Kingdom*. New York: Atheneum Books for Young Readers. (PB)

Collings, Rex. (1993). *A Crash of Rhinoceroses: A Dictionary of Collective Nouns*. Wakefield, RI: Moyer Bell. (NF)

Heller, Ruth. (1991). *A Cache of Jewels and Other Collective Nouns*. New York: Grosset & Dunlap. (PB)

Nathan, Emma. (2000). *What Do You Call a Group of Alligators? (And Other Reptile and Amphibian Groups)*. Woodbridge, CT: Blackbirch Press. (PB)

Nathan, Emma. (2000). *What Do You Call a Group of Butterflies? (And Other Insect Groups)*. Woodbridge, CT: Blackbirch Press. (PB)

Swanson, Diane, and Mariko Ando Spencer. (2006). *A Crash of Rhinos, a Party of Jays: The Wacky Ways We Name Animal Groups*. Illustrated by Mariko Ando Spencer. Toronto, Canada: Annick Press. (PB)

 ## Exploring Cultural Perspectives: Folk and Fairy Tale Variations

Storace, Patricia, and Raul Colon. (2007). *Sugar Cane: A Caribbean Rapunzel*. Illustrated by Raul Colon. New York: Jump at the Sun/Hyperion Books for Children. (FT/PB)

Lead students into a study of cultural perspectives with folk and fairy tale variations. Patricia Storace has rewritten the traditional tale of *Rapunzel* in a Caribbean setting. It is the pregnant wife's craving for sugar cane that gets her husband into trouble when he steals some from the garden of the famous sorceress "Madame Fate." The baby girl, named Sugar Cane, is claimed by the sorceress on her first birthday and imprisoned in a tower. Storace adds some nice cultural artifacts that impact the story: a pet monkey, a coral bracelet, and Caribbean music. The sorceress has voodoo powers, and the handsome "prince" is really a man who has won a music contest and the title of "king." Raul Colon's color illustrations provide a lush visual backdrop for this familiar story.

Activity Suggestions

1. ⊕ *Get it organized:* Form small groups of students who have read variants of the same traditional tale (e.g., a *Cinderella* group, a *Red Riding Hood* group, etc.). Groups should take notes as they discuss how the variations are alike and different. Discuss and/or demonstrate various ways to present information to highlight the similarities and differences. Allow students to choose the method they like best, organize their information, and present it to the group.

2. ⊕⊕ *Personal favorites:* Ask each student to choose a favorite traditional tale, then go to the library and find one or more variations on that tale. Encourage students to explore variations from numerous countries. Students can share their selections in class, either by reading aloud or through small-group discussion.

3. ⊕⊕ *Telling tales:* Folk and fairy tales make wonderful material for storytelling activities. Have each student learn his or her tale and present it orally to the class. Including multiple variations of the same story will allow students to compare them.

4. ⊕⊕ *Give it a try:* Discuss the important story elements of one or more traditional folk or fairy tale. Then, ask students to rewrite the tale and set it in a different culture. Some students may enjoy setting the story in their present-day hometown.

Cross-Curricular Connections

1. ⊕⊕ *Social studies:* Ask students to research the culture featured in a folk or fairy tale variation. What aspects of the culture did the author include? The illustrator? Is the culture presented accurately? What do folk/fairy tales show about a culture? Have students share what they learned by creating informative posters and presenting them to the whole group.

2. ⊕ *Mathematics:* Have students consider the tower in which Rapunzel lived. Ask the whole group to decide what furniture she would have: e.g., a bed, a table and chair, etc. Then, have small groups create a scale drawing of her room with all furniture items cut out to match the scale you specify. Keeping the area as nearly the same as possible, have them try different geometric shapes for the room. Which shape would best accommodate Rapunzel's furniture: a circle, square, triangle, rectangle, or some other shape? Why?

3. ⊕ *The arts:* Read a folk tale aloud without showing the pictures. Then, ask students to illustrate a specific scene. Compare the results across the

class. Ask students to explain the inspiration for their interpretations. Discuss the impact of personal perspective on their artistic choices.

Suggested Text Set for Further Invitations

Baker, E. D. (2002). *The Frog Princess*. New York: Bloomsbury USA. (FYA—novel-length interpretation of *The Frog Prince*).

Daly, Niki. (2006). *Pretty Salma*. New York: Clarion Books. (FT—African version of *Little Red Riding Hood*).

Durst, Sarah Beth. (2007). *Into the Wild: A Novel.* New York: Razorbill. (FYA—includes references to many fairy tales).

Fleischman, Paul, and Julie Paschkis. (2007). *Glass Slipper, Gold Sandal: A Worldwide Cinderella*. Illustrated by Julie Paschkis. New York: Henry Holt. (FT—aspects of multiple countries/cultures included in one story).

Hale, Shannon. (2003). *Goose Girl*. New York: Bloomsbury. (FYA—novel-length interpretation of *Goose Girl*).

Hettinga, Donald R. (2001). *The Brothers Grimm: Two Lives, One Legacy*. New York: Clarion Books. (B)

 ## Traveling Libraries

Ruurs, Margriet. (2005). *My Librarian Is a Camel: How Books Are Brought to Children around the World*. Honesdale, PA: Boyds Mills Press. (NF/PB)

Do you walk (or drive) to your local library? What if the library came to *you*? That happens around the world. There are many ways students in far reaches of the globe gain access to books. Some involve legs (camels, horse-drawn wagons, donkey carts, and elephants), wheels (trucks and wheelbarrows), mail, and water (boats of all sorts). Margriet Ruurs gives us a look at books *not* in buildings. Loaded with photographs that show both the population and transportation of books, we see how truly happy these students are to have access to something many of take for granted. This book is sure to spark wonder about landscapes, populations, and books.

Activity Suggestions

1. �� *Serving up books:* Ruurs shows how thirteen countries are able to provide library services to children in distant areas. Use the map on page 4 to select a country and have students research their libraries.

2. �� *A librarian's many skills:* Librarians featured in the book are both paid and volunteer. Using the descriptions throughout the book, have students list the skills needed by a librarian. They could interview their

school or local librarian and compare what they need to be able to do in the traveling libraries, their school library, and their local library.

3. ☻☻ *Categories by any other name:* Librarians use different systems to categorize books. The most common in the United States is the Dewey Decimal System. Have students browse the school and local libraries to see what they use. Have the students choose one system and categorize your classroom library.

4. ☻☻ *Wanted: Borrowers of good books:* Have students select one of the featured countries and write an advertisement that would be posted to let people know the library is coming soon. Use the information about where they should go to meet the traveling books (such as the dock) and what new titles they might have (one that the students have recently read and can write a "blurb" about). Make the ad persuasive . . . you want people to come to your traveling library.

Cross-Curricular Connections

1. ☻ *Social studies:* The photographs in the book show diverse populations within one setting. Have students check census information to find the nationalities of the students in one of the countries featured. Investigate the languages spoken there, particularly the official language of the country.

2. ☻ *Mathematics:* Obtain a larger map of Finland. Using the map's scale, calculate the mileage the "book-boat" (p. 15) covers during its ten stops. Calculate the weight of the books the boat carries (about six hundred books). How might students estimate that actual weight of all those books?

3. ☻☻ *Science:* The author explains that the truck used in Australia to bring books to children in the Outback is solar powered. Investigate solar power and how the Australians are able to provide energy for computers, lights, stereo, wheelchair lift, and refrigerator. Examine the potential of UPS (uninterrupted power supply) as an alternative to our electrical circuits. Discuss their findings.

Suggested Text Set for Further Invitations

Appelt, Kathi, and Jeanne Cannella Schmitzer. (2001). *Down Cut Shin Creek: The Pack Horse Librarians of Kentucky*. New York: HarperCollins. (NF)

Bankston, John. (2004). *Michael L. Printz and the Story of the Michael L. Printz Award*. Great Achievement Awards. Bear, DE: Mitchell Lane Publishers. (B)

Gonzalez, Lucia M., and Lulu Delacre. (2008). *The Storyteller's Candle: La Velita de los Cuentos*. San Francisco, CA: Children's Book Press. (FPB)

Oppenheim, Joanne. (2006). *Dear Miss Breed: True Stories of the Japanese American Incarceration During World War II and a Librarian Who Made a Difference*. New York: Scholastic. (NF)

Peck, Richard. (2006). *Here Lies the Librarian*. New York: Dial Books. (FYA)

Sanderson, Brandon. (2007). *Alcatraz Versus the Evil Librarians*. Alcatraz Smedry Adventures. New York: Scholastic Press. (FYA)

Winter, Jeanette. (2005). *The Librarian of Basra: A True Story from Iraq*. Orlando, FL: Harcourt. (NF)

 ## Made You Look! Viewing in the Language Arts

Bryan, Kim. (2008). *One Million Things: A Visual Encyclopedia*. New York: DK Publishing. (NF/PB)

This stunning photographic book is sure to stop any student in their tracks. Lush color photographs virtually leap off the page. Viewing demands careful analysis, and this book provides limitless opportunities to explore its pages connected to every area of the curriculum. Sections include nature, human body, science and technology, space, earth, people and places, history, and art and culture. Accompanying each two-page spread are short paragraphs, descriptive callout boxes, captions, labels, terms, and an abundance of information. Its large format (10 inches □ 12 inches) makes it ideal for small groups to share and explore. This book is sure to be the most "in demand" book in your classroom.

Activity Suggestions

1. ☻ *Where do I look?* The photos and print on each two-page spread will no doubt amaze students. The print takes the form of both paragraphs and captions. Have students discover their preference as a page is opened. Where do their eyes go first? Using pages such as 196–197 (North America), where the main paragraph is not in a typical place, ask them to list the order of where their eyes traveled on the pages. Compare student responses. Did they completely miss some sections? Did they look at photos first or print? Discuss the author's approach to help our eyes "travel" around the page.

2. ☻ *Viewing 101:* Part of viewing is the ability to see the basic elements of communication. These include the dot, line, shape, direction, value, hue and saturation, texture, scale, dimension, and motion. Allow each student to select a two-page spread and to report on how each of the elements was or was not met on the pages. For instance, on pages 206–207 (flags), multiple objects are used to display ten country flags. What shapes

are used on all the flags? What colors are dominant? What textures and scale are used?

3. ☺ *A picture is worth a thousand words*: Another important part of viewing is to interpret the images one sees. Cover the large caption on a page and hold the book so students cannot see the print. Ask them to study the images they see and suggest what the "organizing" feature is on those two pages. You can begin simply by showing the birds (pp. 46–47) and progress to more difficult pages, such as extreme living (pp. 224–225). What other objects might they suggest be added to a page?

4. ☺ *Redefining "reference"*: Show any of the pages from the reference section (pp. 281–297). These pages are filled with one-liners (of various size font and direction of print) that give further information for each section of the book. For instance, on one of the art and culture pages, we are told "The **deputy electrician** on a film set is the **'best boy,'** even when she's a girl" (p. 296). Students can engage in several viewing activities on these pages. What is the background for each section? A faint repeating pattern ties into the section; for instance, purple pages with white Saturns are used for space. Why did the author choose to represent that section with that particular background? Next, have the students step back and look at the layout of the print. How is it arranged? How do the font changes attract your eye? Finally, have students read the nuggets of information given (such as on page 290—"Fresh snow is more than *90 percent* trapped air"). How has the author worded the statements? Turn to a page of interest in the book and have students write their own one-line "nuggets" about something they viewed.

Cross-Curricular Connections

1. ☺☺ *Social studies*: In the section "Earth" (pp. 152–189), a two-page spread is devoted to farm crops (pp. 186–187). The information states that some of the crops are from North America, whereas others are from the tropics. Have students locate on a world map where each crop is grown. If the book does not provide the exact location (such as coconuts are said to be in the Pacific Islands, but no location is given for sunflowers), have the students research where they primarily grow. Examine crops in your area or state. What could the students add to the page from their local experiences?

2. ☺ or ☺☺ *Mathematics*: Many of the photographs are life-size. However, some are enlarged and some are reduced, depending on the information on the page. So the picture of the wasp on pages 26–27 (insect anatomy) is

much larger than life. The page does not provide how much bigger. Have students find the actual size of wasps then measure the one in the book and figure the percent of increase. How much has the fire extinguisher on page 114 (color) been reduced to fit on the page? How big is an actual pumpkin pie (page 220, festivals) compared to the one in the book?

3. ☺☺ *The arts:* An entire section of the book deals directly with the arts (pp. 252–279). This section includes a wide spectrum of choices including orchestra, sports, dance, movies, and media. However, a more unusual connection to the arts might be to use the body systems (pp. 68–69). Here, knitted pieces are used to represent the systems of the body (lungs, heart, brain, and so on). Have students use other media to create three-dimensional versions of these organs (or others not on the page). Or, if a student (or someone in their family) can knit or crochet, ask him or her to work with other students to re-create the ones on the page.

Suggested Text Set for Further Invitations

Aguilar, David A. (2007). *Planets, Stars, and Galaxies: A Visual Encyclopedia of Our Universe*. Washington, DC: National Geographic. (NF)

Davies, Andrew, and Igor Siwanowicz. (2008). *Super-Size Bugs*. Sterling. (NF)

Dotz, Warren, Jack Mingo, and George Moyer. (2008). *Firecrackers!: An Eye-Popping Collection of Chinese Firework Art*. Berkeley, CA: Ten Speed Press. (NF)

Lee, Nancy, Lonnie Schlein, and Mitchel Levitas. (2002). *A Nation Challenged: A Visual History of 9/11 and Its Aftermath*. New York: Scholastic Nonfiction. (NF)

Scholastic Reference. (2003). *Scholastic Visual Sports Encyclopedia*. New York: Scholastic Reference. (NF)

Stanchak, John E. (2000). *The Visual Dictionary of the Civil War*. New York: DK Publishing. (NF)

Townsend, John. (2004). *Mysterious Signs*. Chicago, IL: Raintree. (NF)

 ### Playing with Perspective

Temple, Bob. (2008). *The Titanic: An Interactive History Adventure*. You Choose Books. Mankato, MN: Capstone Press. (NF/PB)

According to Mark Twain, *work* and *play* are words used to describe the same thing under differing conditions. This certainly applies to the 2,200 people on the *Titanic* as it sailed from England in 1912. Bob Temple captures the different perspectives of the passengers: some worked, some played. In this clever story, Temple allows the reader to see the trip through the eyes of the three kinds of passengers who traveled together on the ill-fated *Titanic*. We experience the plush elegance afforded to the first-class passengers. Many of them paid thousands of dollars to make the trip. Or we might take the perspective of a poor, third-class passenger, hoping to reach the United States and begin a better life. Or we could be one of the 890-crew members staffing the ship under the leadership of Captain Edward Smith. The book has many choices and begs for multiple readings to follow the events of different passengers. The stories are true, based on the facts gathered about the ship. The book is full of drawings and photographs to not only add to the facts, but to step into the lives of the many passengers of the *Titanic*.

Activity Suggestions

1. ☺☺ *Other paths to consider:* At the back of the book, Temple offers students some further perspectives to consider. Using the questions he provides (such as asking what it might have been like to be the captain who decided to "go down with the ship"), have students write these as narratives to share in class. The *Titanic* Historical Society will provide information about a number of passengers at http://www.titanichistorical society.org.

2. ☺ or ☺☺ *You step into the book:* Using the dialogue in the book, choose a selection that involves multiple voices. Have the students take on the role of such crewmembers as Captain Smith or passenger Hudson Allison. How would they have spoken the words we read? Perspective is not only about the way you see events occurring, but also how you feel about them. Have the students show how the dialogue would have sounded as the others listen to this story come alive.

3. ☺☺ *Wireless then and now:* The wireless operator on the *Titanic* sent distress signals soon after the ship hit the iceberg. He used the newly introduced SOS code. Introduce students to Morse code, having them construct short messages to send and receive by tapping pencils on their desk.

4. ☺☺ *Try your own interactive adventure:* Have small groups of students collaborate to create their own stories with multiple perspectives. Web the possible participants in a stories, then have each student write how the story is "resolved" for each character. For instance, the students could write a story about an upcoming election. The story begins with common information about the election and who is involved. Then, each student chooses to be one person. They write two versions: one in which

the person wins and one in which he loses. Use the notes at the bottom of the pages in *The Titanic* as guides of how to allow the reader to select different options and endings.

Cross-Curricular Connections

1. ⌚ *Social studies:* The *Titanic* is a classic example of class structures. Have students identify the variations in the passengers' experiences based on their social class. How did being in the lower decks compare to staying in the more expensive cabins? How did their purposes for travel differ?

2. ⌚ *Mathematics:* Use information provided in the book, from the *Titanic* historical site, or National Geographic's Time for Kids article http://magma.nationalgeographic.com/ngexplorer/0411/articles/mainarticle.html to create word problems to solve. For instance, if the ship was 882 feet and 6 inches long, how many football fields long is that? The nine decks were 175 feet high, how would it compare to a tall building in your community?

3. ⌚⌚ *Science:* The demise of the *Titanic* was due to hitting an iceberg. The calm seas made it difficult for crew members to see the approaching iceberg. Examine the properties of icebergs. For specific information to explore the science of the *Titanic*, go to http://www.titanicscience.com.

Suggested Text Set for Further Invitations

Brown, Don. (2008). *All Stations! Distress! April 15, 1912, the Day the Titanic Sank*. New York: Flash Point/Roaring Brook Press. (NF)

Catran, Ken. (2006). *Voyage with Jason*. Vancouver, BC: Simply Read Books. (YAF)

Crosbie, Duncan. (2007). *Titanic: The Ship of Dreams*. London: Orchard Books. (NF/pop-up)

Durkee, Sarah. (2006). *The Fruit Bowl Project: A Novel*. New York: Delacorte Press. (FYA)

Fleischman, Paul, and Beppe Giacobbe. (2000). *Big Talk: Poems for Four Voices*. Illustrated by Beppe Giacobbe. Cambridge, MA: Candlewick Press. (P)

Fleischman, Paul, and Judy Pedersen. (1997). *Seedfolks*. New York: HarperCollins. (FYA)

Frost, Helen. (2006). *The Braid*. New York: Farrar, Straus, and Giroux. (FYA)

Myers, Walter Dean. (2004). *Here in Harlem: Poems in Many Voices*. New York: Holiday House. (P)

Other interactive history adventures that provide multiple perspectives are available from the same publisher: *The Battle of Bunker Hill, The California Gold Rush, The Golden Age of Pirates, Irish Immigrants in America,* and *The Underground Railroad*.

Additional Cross-Curricular Connections

Find more language arts activities under these featured social studies books (Chapter 3):

Warriors: All the Truth, Tactics, and Triumphs of History's Greatest Fighters (Harpur, 2007)

Yatandou (Whelan, 2007)

The Brothers' War: Civil War Voices in Verse (Lewis, 2007)

The Many Rides of Paul Revere (Giblin, 2007)

Dear Mr. Rosenwald (Waterford, 2006)

Muhammad (Demi, 2003)

Seven Miles to Freedom: The Robert Smalls Story (Halfmann, 2008)

Ain't Nothing but a Man: My Quest to Find the Real John Henry (Nelson & Aronson, 2008)

Lady Liberty: A Biography. (Rappaport, 2008)

One Well: The Story of Water on Earth (Strauss, 2007)

Find more language arts activities under these featured math books (Chapter 4):

Wild Fibonacci: Nature's Secret Code Revealed (Hulme, 2005)

Great Estimations (Goldstone, 2006)

Knights and Armor (Firth, 2006)

The Great Number Rumble: A Story of Math in Surprising Places (Lee & O'Reilly, 2007)

The World Record Paper Airplane Book (Blackburn & Lammers, 2006)

Go Figure! A Totally Cool Book about Numbers (Ball, 2005)

Show Me the Money: How to Make Cents of Economics (Hall, 2008)

Find more language arts activities under these featured science books (Chapter 5):

Solving Crimes with Trace Evidence (Jeffrey, 2008)

Team Moon: How 400,000 People Landed Apollo 11 on the Moon (Thimmesh, 2006)

The Leaping, Sliding, Sprinting, Riding Science Book: 50 Super Sports Science Activities (Mercer, 2006)

Cave Detectives (Harrison, 2007)

The Down-to-Earth Guide to Global Warming (David & Gordon, 2007)

Ouch! How Your Body Makes It through a Very Bad Day (Walker, 2007)

Cool Stuff 2.0 and How It Works (Woodford & Woodcock, 2007)

The Story of Salt (Kurlansky, 2006)

Into the Volcano: A Volcano Researcher at Work (Donovan-O'Meara, 2005)

Find more language arts activities under these featured arts books (Chapter 6):

How Does the Show Go on? An Introduction to the Theater (Schumacher & Kurtti, 2007)

Kamishibai Man (Say, 2005)

Steel Drumming at the Apollo: The Road to Super Top Dog (Marx, 2007)

Archie's War: My Scrapbook of the First World War (Williams, 2007)

Good Masters! Sweet Ladies! Voices from a Medieval Village (Schlitz, 2007)

The Illustrated Book of Ballet Stories (Newman, 2005)

The Pot That Juan Built (Andrews-Goebel, 2002)

Signing for Kids (Flodin, 2007)

Paper, Scissors, Sculpt! Creating Cut-and-Fold Animals (Gonzales, 2005)

What's the Big Idea? Activities and Adventures in Abstract Art (Raimondo, 2008)

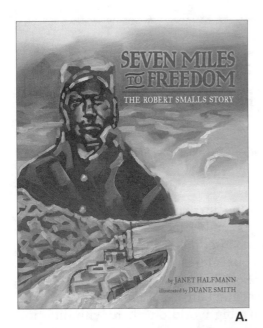

A.

B.

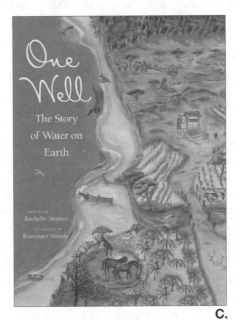

C.

A. *Seven Miles to Freedom: The Robert Smalls Story* by Janet Halfmann; illustrated by Duane Smith. **B.** *Dear Mr. Rosenwald* by Carole Boston Weatherford; illustrated by R. Gregory Christie. **C.** *One Well: The Story of Water on Earth* by Rochelle Strauss; illustrated by Rosemary Woods.

3 Exploring Picture Books in Social Studies

Learning is something students do, NOT something done to students.
—Alfie Kohn

Social studies is one place in the curriculum that we believe students must *do*. Many of us remember memorizing dates, names, and places, only to forget soon after the test was over. Yet we also remember the teacher who ignited our interest in mummies or the Revolutionary War or the Bill of Rights. Social studies is not only a subject but also a way of living. Through this content area, students learn how to be active citizens. They learn there is a big world out there with differing attitudes, cultures, geographies, and perspectives on what is important in one's daily life. We want students to experience the electoral process, not just read about it. We want them to put themselves in a time and place, to see through the eyes of those who lived then and there. A picture book helps you imagine a ride beside Paul Revere, place yourself in a suit of armor, or feel the summer heat of a Mali village.

While textbooks provide the structural guidance for content, picture books can make history come alive. We hear conversations, see primary documents, and observe painted scenes that allow us to travel back in time or step into photographs that capture an important moment. *The Brother's War: Civil War Voices in Verse* (Lewis, 2007) uses black-and-white photos and prose to take us back to the 1800s. Study the day-to-day life in an African village in *Yatandou* (Whelan, 2007) and then compare it to living in your own community. *The Many Rides of Paul Revere* (Giblin, 2007) pulls us into his passion for freedom. We see his views, his many rides, and his legacy along Boston's Freedom Trail. As well, we explore freedom in *Dear Mr. Rosenwald* (Weatherford, 2006) as we are inspired by one student's letter writing to secure funding for a school for African American children. We see what one person can do to change the status quo. Mr. Lowell, a seventh-grade social studies teacher, discovered he could snag the interest of even the most reluctant learner with a history book that is more than just text and pictures. The hands-on approach of *Warriors: All the Truth, Tactics, and Triumphs of History's Greatest Fighters* (Harpur, 2007) provides a look at world history through fold-out pages, pull-out documents, and large maps and charts. Once Mr. Lowell introduced the class to this "must-flip-through-and-see" book, students selected related books from the text set that were of personal interest. Each student read his or her selected book and created a poster using some of the same techniques used by the illustrators of *Warriors* to share what he or she had learned. The book not only made history come alive but also sparked some new interest in further investigations.

Without a doubt, social studies is important for transmitting culture and history. (See Appendix A for the national social studies standards.) If we want it to make a lasting impact on the citizens we teach, then we must make history come alive. The books in this chapter reach out not only to the brain of the learner but also to the heart. We remember what we care about . . . and the lessons learned in these books can provide lasting impressions for middle school students.

Early Civilizations through the Eyes of Warriors

Harpur, James. (2007). *Warriors: All the Truth, Tactics, and Triumphs of History's Greatest Fighters*. New York: Atheneum Books for Young Readers. (NF/PB)

Meet some of the greatest warriors in history. From the 800 BC reign of the Assyrians to the late nineteenth-century Zulus, this book takes us across the globe and through time as we glimpse into the lives of famous warriors. This hardcover, heavy page stock book begs for students to pick it up and flip through it. Filled with maps, photographs, drawings, and special features—such as double fold-out pages, pockets with removable information, multipage booklets, and a large poster of warriors—students will be drawn into the content covered. The visual banquet provided in this book will appeal to a diverse range of learners. Complex in layout, the text in the book ranges from easy reading ("A medieval knight was a noble. His career started as a child, serving as a page in his father's household" [unpaged]) to more advanced discussions ("During medieval times, there emerged in Japan a class of warriors known as 'samurai'. Expert horsemen and masters of archery, they were fierce soldiers who lived by a military code known as 'Bushido' [the way of the warrior]." [unpaged]). This is a truly sumptuous book that will stimulate many discussions.

Activity Suggestions

1. ☉ *Create a classroom "Code of Chivalry"*: Medieval knights were sworn to a code of honor. What "code" should students follow in their treatment

of peers? Discuss what they think is important for all students to follow. Have students create a classroom poster of their code. This is an ideal start-of-the-year activity when you and your students are setting classroom rules and guidelines.

2. ☯ *Where in the world?* Small maps are included in many sections of the book. Use a world map to trace the routes taken by the warriors. Use different color sticky notes to mark the routes. Once these are marked, have students discuss the leaders that were most active in expanding their territory of governance. These leaders can be further investigated in the next activity.

3. ☯☯ *Who's in the news?* Many famous leaders are mentioned in each of the sections. Ask students to do further research on such important historical figures as Alexander the Great, Boudicca and her daughters, Julius Caesar, or Prince Yamato Takeru. Create a large chart with the categories of time period, travel routes, interested facts, and important events. Ask students to contribute information about the leader they investigated. Once the chart is complete, discuss the similarities and differences betweenthese warriors.

4. ☯☯ *Who is Genghis Khan?* Using the famous warriors as "characters," have students consider what they might have been like. Students could create readers' theater scripts (see Appendix B) to present their character. Share these over several days in class or invite other classes in to a production of *Who is Genghis Khan?*

Cross-Curricular Connections

1. ☯☯ *Language arts*: Using the "Roman Military Guide" as a model, write a student manual for your school. This manual could explain to new students how to follow such rules as walking in the hallways, sitting in the cafeteria, or arriving at their locker. Have students interview students in other classes and create a working list of rules. Divide the areas of school (cafeteria, locker area, etc.) and allow small groups to write the text for the guide.

2. ☯☯ *Science*: Investigate how archaeologists discover the remains that inform us about these warriors and the places they lived. Using your school library resources, have students research and list how archaeologists reconstruct sites, such as the Colosseum in Rome. Each student (or pairs of students) should create a list to share that presents the challenges,

time and tools needed, and the resulting findings for a particular archaeological discovery related to the book.

3. ☺ or ☺☺ *The arts*: Explore color used by the various warriors. Have students reproduce through a drawing one of the coats of arms found in the book. Label the drawing, showing the symbolism behind the colors chosen for a knight's coat of arms.

Suggested Text Set for Further Exploration

Lekuton, Joseph L., and Herman J. Viola. (2003). *Facing the Lion: Growing Up Maasai on the African Savanna*. Washington, DC: National Geographic Books. (B)

Mann, Elizabeth. (2006). *The Roman Colosseum*. Wonders of the World Series. New York: Mikaya Press. (NF)

Pearson, Anne. (2000). *Ancient Greece*. Eyewitness Books, 37. New York: DK Children. (NF)

Pierce, Tamora, and Josepha Sherman. (Eds.) (2006). *Young Warriors: Stories of Strength*. New York: Random House Children's Books. (AN/F)

Rumford, James. (2007). *Beowulf: A Hero's Tale Retold*. Boston: Houghton Mifflin. (FT).

Steele, Philip, Penny Bateman, and Norma Rosso. (2000). *The Aztec News*. Cambridge, MA: Candlewick Press. (FPB) (Note: This series includes *The Roman News* by Andrew Langley, *The Greek News* by Anton Powell, *History News: Explorer News* by Michael Johnstone, and many more titles.)

Village Life in Africa (Mali)

Whelan, Gloria, and Peter Sylvada. (2007). *Yatandou*. Tales of the World. Illustrated by Peter Sylvada. Chelsea, MI: Sleeping Bear Press. (FPB)

Read this fictional picture book aloud to provide a snapshot of life in a Malian village. Based on the results of a United Nations program implemented in 350 African villages, the book describes the successful efforts of village women to purchase a machine that will do three hours of backbreaking work in just seconds. As a side effect, the girls and women of the village learn to read and write so they can account for the machine's use. Though the book depicts present-day life, students will be amazed at "how hard many Africans [have] to work to take from the land necessities as simple as a drink of water or a dish of porridge" (author's note). The simple text is filled with interesting cultural references, but Peter Sylvada's gorgeous illustrations steal the show. They fairly shimmer with the summer heat.

Activity Suggestions

1. ☻ *Favorite foods:* Try to find a recipe for bat stew (a favorite food in the story). Then, have students bring recipes for family favorites. Especially request any that have been handed down through generations. Ask students to describe the origins of the recipes they brought.

2. ☻ or ☻☻ *How can we help?* Use the Internet to find out more about the United Nations Development Program that provides villages with grinding machines. What other programs does the U.N. support? Extend this activity by asking students to choose a local cause and outline a way to help. Encourage them to put their project into action.

3. ☻☻ *Time for a change:* Make a timeline showing when various agricultural machines came into use in our country. Where would the "multifunctional platform" (grinding machine) fit on the timeline? Discuss how it compares to the machines used on modern U.S. farms.

4. ☻☻ *Look it up:* Find Mali on a map of Africa. Research the climate, the crops grown there, and the culture. Use this information to evaluate the accuracy of this fictional story.

Cross-Curricular Connections

1. ☻ *Language arts:* In the story, the pounding stick becomes a metaphor for the old way of life. Have students create metaphors to describe things they consider to be outdated. Have them write a paragraph in the style of the story's final page.

2. ☻ or ☻☻ *Mathematics:* This book is a natural for generating math problems. For example, how many seconds are in three hours? If a woman does three hours of work in thirty seconds, what is the percentage of time saved? How much time will six women save? Extend the activity by having students create their own work-related problems for others to solve.

3. ☻☻ *Science:* Discuss the impact of technology on the quality of life in this village. Have students list technological advances that have had a great impact on life in our own country. Choose the greatest technological improvement by having students nominate their favorite. Each nomination should include a justification statement. Those who feel strongly can "campaign" in favor of their choice before the class votes for a winner. Follow up by checking online sources to see what the experts think. For example, the *Popular Mechanics* website (www.popularmechanics.com) presented "The Top 50 Inventions of the Past 50 Years" in December 2005. Do students agree with these choices?

Suggested Text Set for Further Exploration

Burns, Khephra, Leo Dillon, and Diane Dillon. (2001). *Mansa Musa: The Lion of Mali*. Illustrated by Leo and Diane Dillon. San Diego: Harcourt Brace & Co. (B)

Croze, Harvey. (2006). *Africa for Kids: Exploring a Vibrant Continent, 19 Activities*. Chicago, IL: Chicago Review Press. (NF)

Goss, Linda. (2006). *Exploring Mali: A Young Person's Guide to Ancient Civilization*. Norfolk, VA: Maya Publications. (NF)

Masoff, Joy. (2002). *Mali: Land of Gold and Glory*. Waccabuc, NY: Five Ponds Press. (NF)

Murray, Jocelyn, and Brian A. Stewart. (2007). *Africa (Cultural Atlas for Young People)*. New York: Chelsea House. (NF)

Musgrove, Margaret, Leo Dillon, and Diane Dillon. (1976). *Ashanti to Zulu: African Traditions*. Illustrated by Leo and Diane Dillon. New York: Dial Press. (ABC)

Civil War: Brother against Brother

Lewis, J. Patrick. (2007). *The Brothers' War: Civil War Voices in Verse*. Photographs by Civil War photographers. Washington, DC: National Geographic. (P/PB)

Introduce a lesson on the War between the States with this book of poetry. Eloquent text matched with powerful black-and-white photos from the Civil War era will set the stage for learning about families divided by perspectives, loyalties, and sometimes death. Each double-page spread includes a photo and a poem. Accompanying text explains the poem's context and documents the source of the photograph. In verse that speaks in the voices of slaves or abolitionists or wounded soldiers, Lewis examines issues underlying the war. Students will find connections to current events, too, as in the poem *Passing in Review*, in which the author maintains "a civil war breaks men from boys" (p. 26). This book adds an emotional component to a study of the Civil War.

Activity Suggestions

1. ☺ *Dear family:* The book includes two pages with sample letters from soldiers. After students have read them, have them write a return letter to one of the soldiers.

2. ☺☺ *If it happened today:* Help students make connections to the present day. Ask them to match one of Lewis's poems to a photograph and/or news article about a current event. Ask students to write a paragraph ex-

plaining the connection or connections they see between the poem and the photograph they selected. Share poems and paragraphs in small groups.

3. ☺☺ *Is that a fact?* Have students select poems from the book, and then investigate the events that inspired their poems. The next day, group students according to the poems they selected. Groups can discuss which specific words and phrases most clearly represent the facts of the event and which are meant to symbolize the emotional side of war. Then, ask each student to select one word and write a short poem about war showing either factual or emotional aspects.

4. ☺☺ *Civil War portraits:* The poem *I Am Fast in My Chains* (p. 17) is paired with a photo portrait of Frederick Douglass. Ask students to select a key individual from the Civil War, research that individual, and create a "portrait" in words—either poetry or prose.

Cross-Curricular Connections

1. ☺ or ☺☺ *Language arts:* Provide a selection of current newspapers or news-oriented magazines. Allow students to choose one current event photograph, decide whose perspectives are represented in the photo, and write a poem from that person's or group's perspective.

2. ☺ *Mathematics:* The number of casualties on each side of the war was horrendous. What percentage of Union soldiers died? Confederate soldiers? Have students check Internet statistics to see how both numbers compare to percentages of casualties from more recent wars.

3. ☺ *The arts:* Ask students to bring in a photograph that speaks to them on an emotional level. Display the photos. Have small groups of students discuss the emotional impact of each photo and list descriptive words that express that impact.

Suggested Text Set for Further Exploration

Armstrong, Jennifer, and Mathew B. Brady. (2005). *Photo by Brady: A Picture of the Civil War.* New York: Atheneum Books for Young Readers. (NF)

Bolotin, Norm. (2002). *Civil War A to Z: A Young Reader's Guide to Over 100 People, Places, and Points of Importance.* New York: Dutton Children's Books. (ABC)

Hoose, Phillip M. (2001). *We Were There, Too! Young People in U.S. History.* New York: Farrar, Straus, and Giroux. (NF)

Hughes, Pat, and Ken Stark. (2007). *Seeing the Elephant: A Story of the Civil War.* Illustrated by Ken Stark. New York: Farrar, Straus, and Giroux. (FPB)

Mills, Claudia. (2008). *The Totally Made-Up Civil War Diary of Amanda MacLeish*. New York: Farrar, Straus, and Giroux. (FYA)

Woodruff, Elvira. (2000). *Dear Austin: Letters from the Underground Railroad*. Illustrated by Nancy Carpenter. New York: Dell Yearling. (FYA)

Revolutionary U.S. Studies

Giblin, James Cross. (2007). *The Many Rides of Paul Revere*. New York: Scholastic Press. (B/PB)

Many students know of the "midnight ride of Paul Revere," but do they know there were *many* rides? Giblin begins with the immigration of Revere's father from France. Persecuted for his religion, Apollos Rivoire moved to America in 1715. After opening his business of silver and goldsmithing, Apollos changed his name to Paul Revere. His first son was named after him, and thus began the life of the Paul Revere who grew up to be an integral figure in the Sons of Liberty, the Revolutionary War, and the Continental Congress. This carefully researched book follows Revere's life and the key role he played in this country's separation from England. Highly illustrated with maps and photographs of engravings and silver work, we learn of the many talents and patriotic passions of Paul Revere. Included are a current map of Boston's Freedom Trail, Longfellow's *Paul Revere's Ride*, and a detailed timeline.

Activity Suggestions

1. ☺☺ *Famous character trading cards*: Have students create cards about each of the important historical figures mentioned in the book. Students try to guess what person the other student has described by exchanging and reading cards. Multiple copies could be made to play various matching card games. (See Appendix B).

2. ☺☺ *A rider's guide*: Using the information about Revere's various rides, have students create travel brochures that invite peers to reenact the travel routes he took. Maps, scenic information, and possible harrowing experiences should be included.

3. ☺ *You said, he said*: Using Henry Wadsworth Longfellow's *Paul Revere's Ride*, create, as a class or individually, a Venn diagram (see Appendix B) of the events of April 18, 1775, as described in the book and in the poem. Have students discuss the similarities and differences they observed in the construction of the diagram.

4. ☉ *No taxation without representation!* One of the memorable quotes from this time period spurred the colonists to break free of England. Ask students to create cause-and-effect charts (see Appendix B) that analyze the incidents that upset the colonists and the resulting actions. Use the book to cite the pages the students used when completing the chart to demonstrate their understanding of cause and effect.

Cross-Curricular Connections

1. ☉ *Language arts:* Many words and sayings we use today come from Revolutionary times. Have students investigate and share the origin and meaning of such words as *minuteman, turncoat,* "lock, stock, and barrel," "big wig," "bury the hatchet," "climb into bed," "sleep tight," and "toe the line." Create a bulletin board of these sayings that can be added to as students find other examples in their readings. (http://www.phrases. org.uk/ is a useful resource.)

2. ☉ *Mathematics:* Several parts of this book lend themselves to a math focus. Examples might include: (a) using the maps to trace routes; how many miles did Revere ride? (b) When going by horseback, how many miles an hour did he travel? When going by foot? Have students write a paragraph describing the mathematical functions they needed to use to answer each question.

3. ☉☉ *The arts:* Students could research and/or replicate some of the art forms mentioned in the book (engraving, oil painting, watercolor, miniature painting with a single hair of a brush). Use your curriculum to select the appropriate media. A local artist may be willing to show the students a form that you cannot duplicate in school (such as silversmithing). Contact your local arts council for help.

Suggested Text Set for Further Exploration

Haislip, Phyllis Hall. (2005). *Divided Loyalties: A Revolutionary War Fifer's Story.* Shippensburg, PA: White Mane Kids. (FYA)

Longfellow, Henry Wadsworth, and Christopher H. Bing. (2001). *The Midnight Ride of Paul Revere.* Engravings by Christopher Bing. Brooklyn, NY: Handprint. (P)

Marrin, Albert. (2001). *George Washington & the Founding of a Nation.* New York: Dutton Children's Books. (B)

Niz, Xavier W., and Brian Bascle. (2006). *Paul Revere's Ride.* Graphic Library. Illustrated by Brian Bascle. Mankato, MN: Capstone Press. (PB)

Turner, Ann Warren. (2003). *Love Thy Neighbor: The Tory Diary of Prudence Emerson.* Dear America. New York: Scholastic. (FYA)

Winnick, Karen B. (2000). *Sybil's Night Ride*. Honesdale, PA: Boyds Mills Press. (NF)

Schools: Separate and Unequal

Weatherford, Carole Boston, and R. Gregory Christie. (2006). *Dear Mr. Rosenwald*. Illustrated by R. Gregory Christie. New York: Scholastic Press. (FPB)

In the 1920s, schools in the southern states were segregated. Julius Rosenwald, president of Sears, Roebuck and Co., was inspired by Booker T. Washington to fund schools for African American children. This is the story of one such school, told from one child's point of view. "How on earth will poor people find money to give away?" asks Ovella when she learns that the community must raise part of the money for the school. Yet over a period of a year, they do just that. When the children proudly enter their brand-new school, they find out what their first assignment will be: to write a letter of thanks to Mr. Rosenwald. Colorful illustrations by R. Gregory Christie add a cultural flair to this interesting book.

Activity Suggestions

1. ☻ *To whom it may concern:* Have students write letters to someone whose efforts have benefited their school. Students can use Ovella's letter from the book as an inspiration for writing their own.

2. ☻ *Across the miles:* Set up opportunities for students to have pen pals or e-pals in other school systems across the country or even in other lands. Ask them to find out what schools are like in other locales. (This activity may be repeated and/or ongoing.)

3. ☻ or ☻☻ *School supplies:* Children in this story had only hand-me-down materials from the white school. Assign students to find out about current school budgets. Using the data they find, create a table comparing the expenses of several local school systems, as well as selected districts across the state. Note how much it costs to educate each student across various school districts. To extend this, ask students to interview family members on whether and/or why they think a difference in school expenditures is fair.

4. ☻☻ *Building up education:* Investigate the Rosenwald schools on the Internet and learn about efforts to preserve them. Invite students to participate in preservation efforts. Involve them in social action by cooperatively developing and implementing a fund-raising activity to help support these schools.

Cross-Curricular Connections

1. ☑☑ *Language arts:* Booker T. Washington was the inspiration for the Rosenwald schools. Have students find out more about him and write bio-poems (see Appendix B) that tell about his life. Share them orally.

2. ☑ *Mathematics:* Using the Internet, help students find out how much a Rosenwald School actually cost, then figure out what percent Mr. Rosenwald donated. Have students create word problems related to the cost of land, materials, and school supplies, and then write equations and find the solutions.

3. ☑ *The arts:* Compare the art of R. Gregory Christie with that of Jacob Lawrence, author/illustrator of several books that reflect African American culture and history. Discuss as a group. Poll students as to which they like best and why.

Suggested Text Set for Further Exploration

Alexander, Elizabeth, Marilyn Nelson, and Floyd Cooper. (2007). *Miss Crandall's School for Young Ladies and Little Misses of Color: Poems.* Illustrated by Floyd Cooper. Honesdale, PA: Boyds Mills Press. (P)

Bridges, Ruby. (1999). *Through My Eyes.* New York: Scholastic Press. (B/PB)

Jurmain, Suzanne. (2005). *The Forbidden Schoolhouse: The True and Dramatic Story of Prudence Crandall and Her Students.* Boston: Houghton Mifflin. (NF)

Morrison, Toni. (2004). *Remember: The Journey to School Integration.* Boston: Houghton Mifflin. (NF)

Rodman, Mary Ann. (2004). *Yankee Girl.* New York: Farrar, Straus, and Giroux. (FYA)

Swain, Gwenyth, and Larry Johnson. (2006). *A Hunger for Learning: A Story about Booker T. Washington.* A Creative Minds Biography. Illustrated by Larry Johnson. Minneapolis, MN: Millbrook Press. (B/PB)

 ## Broadening Perspectives on World Religions

Demi. (2003). *Muhammad.* New York: Margaret K. McElderry. (B/PB)

Kick off a study of world religions with this gorgeous biography of Muhammad by Demi. This clear and concise history of the Prophet follows his life from birth in the year 570 CE, through his "Night of Power" and the years of his revelations, and on to his death in 632 CE. To accompany the text, the award-winning author/illustrator has created stunning color illustrations with a traditional Islamic flavor. Because that tradition prohibits the Prophet Muhammad from being depicted, the author effectively represents him as a golden silhouette. Authenticity is emphasized by a foreword written by an Islamic scholar, a postscript clarifying the essence of Islam, and a useful bibliography. But it is Demi's amazing illustrations that draw in the reader and steal the show.

Activity Suggestions

1. ☻ *Local religious practices:* Check the Yellow Pages to see which religions are represented locally. Where is the nearest Christian church? Jewish synagogue? Could a member of the Islamic faith find a place to worship locally? Use the Internet to see how far he or she would have to travel. What about a Buddhist?

2. ☻ *What time is it?* Students may be accustomed to seeing the abbreviations BC or AD following dates. This is a good time for them to learn about CE (Common, Christian, or Current Era) and BCE (Before Common, Christian, or Current Era). These updated terms show sensitivity to non-Christian cultures.

3. ☻ or ☻☻ *Commonalities:* Students will gain perspectives on world religions by looking for commonalities among them. Have small groups research the tenets of the five major religions (Buddhism, Christianity, Hinduism, Islam, Judaism). Jigsaw group members (See Appendix B) to share information and help all students compare the foundations of each faith. The length of time required will depend on availability of computers, how much detail you require, etc.

4. ☻☻ *Comparing time frames:* To put Muhammad's life in temporal context, have small groups create timelines to represent the lives of notable religious figures (e.g., Muhammad, Buddha, Jesus, etc.). Timelines should be done according to a single prescribed format and include world events. On another day, line up the timelines to see when these individuals lived. Can the students draw any conclusions? Discuss the impact of world events on religion and vice versa.

Cross-Curricular Connections

1. ☻ *Language arts:* Throughout the book, Muhammad is portrayed as a silhouette. As part of viewing, have students examine each of the illustrations and suggest what role it plays in the scene.

2. ☻ *Mathematics:* On the Internet, students can find out the number of people in the world, as well as the number of individuals practicing each

religion. What percentage of the world's population embraces each faith? Have students develop different kinds of graphs to represent the percentages. A similar activity will give a picture of U.S. religious practices. Do the percentages follow the same patterns? Which religions are most highly represented in the United States?

3. ☺☺ *The arts:* Early Christian art was often created in the form of a triptych, a hinged panel painting divided into three sections. Ask students to research this art form. Then have them create their own triptychs (related to religion or another topic).

Suggested Text Set for Further Exploration

Buller, Laura. (2005). *A Faith Like Mine: A Celebration of the World's Religions— Seen through the Eyes of Children*. New York: DK Publishing. (NF)

Cohn, Janice, and Bill Farnsworth. (1995). *The Christmas Menorahs: How a Town Fought Hate*. Illustrated by Bill Farnsworth. Morton Grove, IL: Albert Whitman. (NF)

Cooper, Ilene. (2004). *Sam I Am*. New York: Scholastic Press. (FYA)

Holm, M. S. (2007). *How Mohammed Saved Miss Liberty*. New York: Great West. (FYA)

Langley, Myrtle. (2005). *Religion*. Eyewitness Books. New York: DK Publishing. (NF)

Macaulay David. (1981). *Cathedral: The Story of Its Construction*. Boston: Houghton Mifflin. (NF)

Macaulay David. (2003). *Mosque*. Boston: Houghton Mifflin. (NF)

 Journeys: Marching to the Drumbeats of Freedom

Halfmann, Janet, and Duane Smith. (2008). *Seven Miles to Freedom: The Robert Smalls Story*. Illustrated by Duane Smith. New York: Lee & Low Books. (B/PB)

Born a slave in South Carolina, Robert Smalls yearned for freedom. As he grew into young adulthood, his dependability earned him a position of trust. He became a "wheelman," the name given to black boat pilots in the South. It was the Civil War that presented him with an opportunity to escape to the North. He and his crew stole their wood-burning steamboat, secretly picked up their families who were waiting on shore, and made a harrowing journey past numerous Confederate forts. Their gamble paid off when they crossed into Union-held waters. Robert later became the first African American captain of a U.S. vessel, helped to write the constitution of South Carolina, and was elected to Congress. He also purchased the home of his former master. Duane Smith's color illustrations provide interest, while an afterword and list of sources add authenticity to this amazing story about a flight to freedom.

Activity Suggestions

1. ☺ *The importance of literacy:* Slaves rarely were allowed to learn to read and write. Discuss why that happened. Ask students to list all the ways they use the skills of reading and writing. Share and combine the lists.

2. ☺☺ *Help wanted:* Robert Smalls traveled on a steamboat when he made his way north to freedom. However, many more slaves traveled by way of the Underground Railroad. These slaves were dependent on others to help them escape, but most of these "others" did not become famous. This is a great opportunity to discuss the many unsung heroes who help others simply because it is the right thing to do. Have students write essays about these "unsung heroes." Share orally.

3. ☺☺ *Cite the evidence:* Robert Smalls is quoted as saying, "My race needs no special defense, for the past history of them in this country proves them to be the equal of any people. All they need is an equal chance in the battle of life" (Halfmann, 2008, unpaged). Ask students to find evidence (e.g., via the Internet, reference books, etc.) that Smalls was correct. Have them share their findings orally. Discuss what is meant by "an equal chance" in life.

4. ☺☺ *The name game:* The *Major General Robert Smalls* was the first U.S. Army vessel to be named after an African American. Have students research the names of other ships that were named after people. For what individuals were they named? What were the honorees' accomplishments? Have students describe the commonalities of these individuals. Create a group table listing the names of the ships, the honorees, and their accomplishments.

Cross-Curricular Connections

1. ☺☺ *Language arts:* Ask students to write a news report of the escape of Robert Smalls as a reporter might have written it when it actually happened. Ask them to consider whether reports of the day would have had all the facts. How would they get their information? How would their report be different if they wrote it today? Discuss technological changes that affect how we now report and receive the news.

2. ☺ or ☺☺ *Science:* There are multimedia science sites that show the

power of steam, such as http://www.howstuffworks.com. Search for steam engine animation and find the two science-related articles. Let students view the animations, and then discuss the pros and cons of steam engines versus other forms of power. To extend this activity, assign students to find out more about the uses of steam power and have them report back to the class.

3. ☺☺ *The arts:* Show students a clip from the movie *Glory* (Tristar, 1989). Discuss how the music affects the mood. Have small groups of students write scenes from Halfmann's book. Ask them to suggest music that would be appropriate for the mood of their scene.

Suggested Text Set for Further Exploration

Carson, Mary Kay. (2005). *The Underground Railroad for Kids: From Slavery to Freedom with 21 Activities.* Chicago: Chicago Review Press. (NF)

Kamma, Anne, and Pamela Johnson. (2004). *. . . If You Lived When There Was Slavery in America.* Illustrated by Pamela Johnson. New York: Scholastic. (NF)

Levitin, Sonia. (2000). *Dream Freedom.* San Diego: Silver Whistle. (FYA)

Nelson, Marilyn, and Pamela Espeland. (2004). *Fortune's Bones: The Manumission Requiem.* New York: Handprint. (P)

Taylor, Yuval. (2005). *Growing Up in Slavery: Stories of Young Slaves as Told by Themselves.* Chicago, IL: Lawrence Hill Books. (B)

Weatherford, Carole Boston, and Kadir Nelson. (2006). *Moses: When Harriet Tubman Led Her People to Freedom.* Illustrated by Kadir Nelson. New York: Hyperion Books for Children. (B)

History Detectives: Searching for Knowledge and Justice

Nelson, Scott Reynolds, and Marc Aronson. (2008). *Ain't Nothing but a Man: My Quest to Find the Real John Henry.* Washington, DC: National Geographic. (NF/PB)

Historian Scott Reynolds Nelson was trying to find out more about the 40,000 African American men who helped build the railroads through America's southern states. With little written evidence of their existence, he turned to songs that were passed down through generations. One of these was the folk song *John Henry* in its many versions. The book chronicles Nelson's efforts to determine whether there was a real John Henry. Students will be fascinated with his account of the old postcard that led him to the truth about this legendary hero who "died with a hammer in his hand." They also will learn that research can bring more than knowledge. It can bring justice. Historic photos make the topic real, while a wonderful two-page appendix by Marc Aronson details the stages of research so students can become historical researchers, too.

Activity Suggestions

1. ☺ *It's in the song—or is it?* To introduce this book, play a version of the old favorite folk song. Ask students to write down a description of how they think John Henry looked. When the text of the book is read, have them note the author's description. Discuss how the two are different. What does this say about tall-tale heroes?

2. ☺ or ☺☺ *Folk heroes:* Have students research other folk heroes. Possibilities could include Paul Bunyan, Pecos Bill, Annie Oakley, Johnny Appleseed, Davy Crockett, and the like. Ask students to focus on whether these were real people. How much of what is written in the stories and songs is true? When were these tales written? What do they reveal about the times? This could be done in or out of class.

3. ☺☺ *Primary sources:* Bring in some primary sources—old family photos, diaries, etc. Discuss their importance to the study of history. Ask students to bring in additional primary sources. Put students in small groups to look at these items. Have them list what they can learn from their assigned item or items. Can they draw any interpretations about the time in which the source was generated? What can they learn about the same time period from secondary sources?

4. ☺☺ *History detectives:* Have students investigate a local puzzle (e.g., whether a suspected Underground Railroad site was real). Some things they can consider are: How can they use Aronson's six stages to help them? Are primary sources available? What secondary sources can they use? Have them report on their findings.

Cross-Curricular Connections

1. ☺ or ☺☺ *Language arts:* Discuss how certain personal qualities are exaggerated to create a tall tale. Then, have students place themselves in a tall-tale adventure by writing an exaggerated account of their own lives. It would be fun to have students share these orally on another day.

2. ☺ *Mathematics:* Get a 10-pound weight so students can imagine what it would be like to swing a 10-pound track hammer all day long. If John Henry raised his hammer just once a minute for eight hours, how many cumulative pounds did he lift in a day? The author is unsure how heavy

John Henry's hammer was. How many pounds did he lift if the hammer weighed 9 pounds? 12 pounds? 20 pounds?

3. ☺☺ *The arts:* Compare multiple versions of the John Henry folk song. Why are there so many? Let students choose their favorite and learn to sing it. A hammer rhythmically struck on metal will make an appropriate accompaniment and allow students to hear how songs helped workers keep up the rhythm of work. (Students may wish to suggest other sound effects as well.) Movement to the music (e.g., swinging a hammer overhead to strike a "nail" at ground level) will let them imagine the fatigue of the workers after many hours of toil.

Suggested Text Set for Further Exploration

Krull, Kathleen, and Allen Garns. (2003). *I Hear America Singing: Folk Songs for American Families with CD.* Illustrated by Allen Garns. New York: Knopf. (AN—Folk Songs)

Lester, Julius, and Jerry Pinkney. (1994). *John Henry.* Illustrated by Jerry Pinkney. New York: Dial Books. (FT)

Myers, Christopher, and Zora Neale Hurston (2005). *Lies and Other Tall Tales.* Illustrated by Christopher Myers. New York: HarperCollins. (FT)

Nelson, Peter. (2002). *Left for Dead: A Young Man's Search for Justice for the U.S.S. Indianapolis.* New York: Delacorte Press. (NF)

Nelson, Scott Reynolds. (2006). *Steel Drivin' Man: John Henry: The Untold Story of an American Legend.* New York: Oxford University Press. (NF)

Osborne, Mary Pope, and Michael McCurdy. (1991). *American Tall Tales.* Illustrated by Michael McCurdy. New York: Knopf. (AN/FT)

 ## Symbol of Freedom: Coming to America

Rappaport, Doreen, and Matt Taveres. (2008). *Lady Liberty: A Biography.* Illustrated by Matt Tavares. Cambridge, MA: Candlewick Press. (NF/PB)

Author Doreen Rappaport creates a "biography" of the Statue of Liberty that begins with a vision and proceeds through the steps that were necessary to make that vision a reality. Each double-page spread includes a lovely color illustration. The accompanying text gives the perspective of an individual who had some interest in the creation of the statue—the designer, the builder, the publisher who challenged his readers to help pay for the statue's base, etc. Many of these stories are told in the first person, which helps the author bring this story to life. Full-color pictures by Matt Tavares (including one that folds out to show Lady Liberty's impressive size) capture the spirit of the statue and what it stands for. Back material includes statue dimensions, a timeline of events, author and illustrator notes, and a list of sources.

Activity Suggestions

1. ☺☺ *Representations of freedom:* The Statue of Liberty is an important monument to freedom. Assign students to research other monuments (e.g., The Washington Monument, Mount Rushmore, monuments dedicated to soldiers from various wars, etc.). Discuss what makes each of them special and how each contributes to the concept of freedom in our country.

2. ☺ or ☺☺ *Welcome:* Share Emma Lazarus's poem and discuss its meaning. Extend this by asking students (or small groups) to write their own messages of welcome for new students. Share these in class. Have an interested group use their word-processing skills to prepare a welcoming brochure featuring these messages, as well as important information about the school.

3. ☺☺ *We are all Americans:* The Statue of Liberty became an icon for immigrants arriving at Ellis Island. Assign students to research immigration statistics for various time periods (e.g., ten- to twenty-five-year intervals). What were the most common countries of origin in each time period? The next day, during a whole-group presentation of their findings, discuss what trends they found and the reasons for those trends.

4. ☺ or ☺☺ *What do you know?* Immigrants who wanted to become citizens had to be prepared to answer a list of questions. Have small groups create lists of questions they think should be included. Then, provide a list of the real questions. Ask students to compare their suggested questions with the actual ones. To extend this activity, have students interview family members and find out what questions they would include.

Cross-Curricular Connections

1. ☺☺ *Language arts:* An excerpt from Emma Lazarus's poem "The New Colossus" is an important feature of the Statue of Liberty. Obtain a copy of the poem. Have students rewrite the poem in their own words. The next day, discuss the poem's meaning and why it is a fitting quotation to use for this purpose.

2. ☺☺ *Mathematics:* The "Statue of Liberty Dimensions" page contains numerous opportunities for mathematical operations. For example, students could calculate the cost of the pedestal per inch. They could compare the weight (in fractions or percentages) to the weight of other

heavy objects (e.g., a car). They could figure how many Statues of Liberty would reach from the earth to the moon. Let students generate their own problems using these numbers.

3. 😊😊 *The arts:* Sculptor August Bartholdi visualized the Statue of Liberty as we see it today. Discuss Bartholdi's vision and then ask students to draw their own symbol of liberty—as a man, a child, an animal or object, a woman dressed/posed differently, or even a group. Discuss their designs. To extend this activity, students may create three-dimensional views of their designs from clay.

Suggested Text Set for Further Exploration

Bateman, Teresa, and John O'Brien. (2001). *Red, White, Blue, and Uncle Who? The Stories Behind Some of America's Patriotic Symbols.* Illustrated by John O'Brien. New York: Holiday House. (NF)

Cheney, Lynne V., and Robin Preiss-Glassner. (2002). *America: A Patriotic Primer.* Illustrated by Robin Preiss-Glasser. New York: Simon & Schuster Books for Young Readers. (ABC)

Curlee, Lynn. (2003). *Liberty.* New York: Aladdin Paperbacks. (NF)

Hochain, Serge. (2004). *Building Liberty: A Statue Is Born.* Washington, DC: National Geographic. (NF)

Katz, Bobbi, and Nina Crews. (2000). *We the People: Poems.* Illustrated by Nina Crews. New York: Greenwillow Books. (P)

Keenan, Sheila, and Ann Boyajian. (2004). *O, Say Can You See? American Symbols, Landmarks, and Inspiring Words.* Illustrated by Ann Boyajian. New York: Scholastic Reference. (NF)

Peacock, Louise, and Walter Krudrop. (2007). *At Ellis Island: A History in Many Voices.* Illustrated by Walter Lyon Krudop. New York: Atheneum Books for Young Readers. (NF)

Sandler, Martin W. (2004). *Island of Hope: The Story of Ellis Island and the Journey to America.* New York: Scholastic. (NF)

 ## Water: Supporting Life in Our World

Strauss, Rochelle, and Rosemary Woods. (2007). *One Well: The Story of Water on Earth.* Illustrated by Rosemary Woods. Toronto, ON: Kids Can Press. (NF/PB)

"The water you drink today may have rained down on the Amazon rainforest five years ago" (p. 8). But long before that, it may have been part of an underground river or even been consumed by a dinosaur. With this intriguing information, Strauss begins her explanation of how the amount of water on earth remains unchanged. It is, as the title suggests, part of "one well." A series of two-page layouts explore such topics as freshwater versus saltwater, who has access to water, demands on the earth's water supply, and pollution. Also included are conservation suggestions, a note to parents and teachers, and an index for easy reference. Color illustrations by Rosemary Woods add interest and visual information. This is one book that lends itself well to reading just a few pages at a time.

Activity Suggestions

1. ☺ *On the map:* As a whole group, study maps to help students see the relationships between water and the growth of modern cities. Discuss the conclusions they can draw. Then have them write journal entries about what would happen if a community were permanently deprived of water.

2. ☺ *Making choices:* Find out how much water your school uses in a month. Brainstorm ways water can be conserved. Have students suggest schoolwide conservation measures. As a class, choose one of them. Encourage students to be agents for change by taking steps to implement it.

3. ☺☺ *Taking shape:* Ask students to consider the impact of water on history. Each student selects an ancient civilization to study and makes a poster to show what they have learned about how water has "shaped" the course of history. Students can share their posters on another day.

4. ☺☺ *Water use:* Students may be familiar with efforts to eliminate too much energy use. Discuss the ways individuals use water at home. Have them research how much water is used per minute in a shower, to wash hands, to brush teeth, etc. Then, ask them to calculate and graph how much water they use in a given day. Compare graphs and draw conclusions about how water could be conserved.

Cross-Curricular Connections

1. ☺ *Language arts:* Have students read *The Rime of the Ancient Mariner* by Samuel Coleridge. Discuss the significance of water in this story poem.

2. ☺ or ☺☺ *Mathematics:* According to the book, the average person drinks the equivalent of a backyard swimming pool of water in his or her life. How much water is that? Provide photos of various swimming pools and include the dimensions. Have students calculate the volume of each one. Compare results to see which pool holds the most water. For more able students, add challenge by including oddly shaped swimming pools or ask students to calculate the volume of home pools or local public pools.

3. ⏰⏰ *Science:* Investigate the extreme power of water by researching hurricanes, tsunamis, and monsoons. Then, design an experiment to show what damage even a little water can do through freezing (e.g., fill empty soft drink cans with water; seal them and put them in the freezer. See how long it takes for the can to become deformed or even to rupture).

Suggested Text Set for Further Exploration

Cameron, Anne, and Nelle Olsen. (1987). *Raven Returns the Water.* Illustrated by Nelle Olsen. Madeira Park, BC: Harbour. (FT)

Fridell, Ron. (2008). *Earth-Friendly Energy.* Minneapolis, MN: Lerner Publications. (NF)

Green, Jen. (2005). *Saving Water.* Improving Our Environment. Milwaukee, WI: Gareth Stevens. (NF)

Hewitt, Sally. (2009). *Using Water.* The Green Team. New York: Crabtree. (NF)

Langley, Andrew. (2006). *Hurricanes, Tsunamis, and Other Natural Disasters.* Kingfisher Knowledge Series. Boston: Kingfisher. (NF)

Singer, Marilyn, and Meilo So. (2003). *How to Cross a Pond: Poems about Water.* Illustrated by Meilo So. New York: Knopf. (P)

Woods, Michael, and Mary B. Woods. (2007). *Droughts.* Minneapolis, MN: Lerner Publications. (NF)

Additional Cross-Curricular Connections

Find more social studies activities under these featured language arts books (Chapter 2):

Lucy Maud Montgomery: The Author of Anne of Green Gables (Wallner, 2006)

Louis Sockalexis: Native American Baseball Pioneer (Wise, 2007)

How to Write Stories: Pin Your Ideas to the Page (Warren, 2007)

The Girl's Like Spaghetti: Why, You Can't Manage without Apostrophes! (Truss, 2007)

You Let the Cat Out of the Bag! (And Other Crazy Animal Sayings) (Klingel, 2008)

A Crossing of Zebras: Animal Packs in Poetry (Maddox, 2008)

Sugar Cane: A Caribbean Rapunzel (Storace, 2007)

My Librarian Is a Camel: How Books Are Brought to Children around the World (Ruurs, 2005)

One Million Things: A Visual Encyclopedia (Byran, 2008)

The Titanic: An Interactive History Adventure (Temple, 2008)

Find more social studies activities under these featured math books (Chapter 4):

Twenty-One Elephants and Still Standing (Prince, 2005)

Skyscraper (Curlee, 2007)

Great Estimations (Goldstone, 2006)

Knights and Armor (Firth, 2006)

Go Figure! A Totally Cool Book about Numbers (Ball, 2005)

Show Me the Money: How to Make Cents of Economics (Hall, 2008)

A Very Improbable Story (Einhorn, 2008)

Find more social studies activities under these featured science books (Chapter 5):

Solving Crimes with Trace Evidence (Jeffrey, 2008)

Team Moon: How 400,000 People Landed Apollo 11 on the Moon (Thimmesh, 2006)

Cave Detectives (Harrison, 2007)

Amazing Leonardo da Vinci Inventions You Can Build Yourself (Anderson, 2006)

Into the Volcano: A Volcano Researcher at Work (Donovan-O'Meara, 2005)

Find more social studies activities under these featured arts books (Chapter 6):

How Does the Show Go on? An Introduction to the Theater (Schumacher & Kurtti, 2007)

Kamishibai Man (Say, 2005)

Steel Drumming at the Apollo: The Road to Super Top Dog (Marx, 2007)

Archie's War: My Scrapbook of the First World War (Williams, 2007)

Good Masters! Sweet Ladies! Voices from a Medieval Village (Schlitz, 2007)

The Illustrated Book of Ballet Stories (Newman, 2005)

The Pot That Juan Built (Andrews-Goebel, 2002)

Signing for Kids (Flodin, 2007)

Paper, Scissors, Sculpt! Creating Cut-and-Fold Animals (Gonzales, 2005)

What's the Big Idea? Activities and Adventures in Abstract Art (Raimondo, 2008)

A.

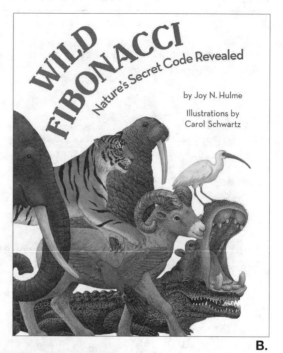

B.

C.

A. *Twenty-One Elephants and Still Standing* by April Jones Prince; illustrated by François Roca. **B.** *Wild Fibonacci* by Joy N. Hulme; illustrated by Carol Schwartz. **C.** *The Great Number Rumble* by Cora Lee and Gillian O'Reilly; illustrated by Virginia Gray.

4 Picture Book Solutions for Mathematics

The real purpose of books is to trap the mind into doing its own thinking.
—Christopher Morley

Math is everywhere in our world. Without it, we can't estimate how many miles a car can travel on a tank of gas, figure out how much time to allow for a crosstown trip, or purchase the correct amount of wood to build a fence. Nearly every job requires knowledge and use of mathematics in some way. Unfortunately, many students don't understand that math is more than a subject to study in school. They don't see it as a real-world tool to use on a daily basis.

Picture books offer solutions for math class dilemmas. One problem for math teachers is that some students don't like the subject. However, those same students may be more than willing to read or listen to a story. In this case, using picture books makes math more palatable and may pique their interest in mathematical concepts.

Picture books also offer another way to look at math. Useful picture books for math classes can fall into two categories (Giorgis & Hartman, 2000). In some books, math is the primary focus. The reader explores a skill or concept through the text and accompanying illustrations. For example, in *Wild Fibonacci: Nature's Secret Code Revealed* (Hulme, 2005), students expand their knowledge of the Fibonacci sequence. *Great Estimations* by Goldstone (2006) offers numerous techniques for generating accurate estimates. For those who don't see the value of math, teachers can recommend *The Great Number Rumble: A Story of Math in Surprising Places* (Lee & O'Reilly, 2007), a humorous story that may encourage an attitude adjustment.

Math class can also focus on real-world topics, with a book providing context for applying mathematical principles. Among examples that explore topics with plenty of practical math applications are *Knights and Armor* (Firth, 2006) and *Twenty-One Elephants and Still Standing* (Prince, 2005), a book about testing the weight limits of the Brooklyn Bridge. After sharing some or all of the text, teachers can assign specific problems or encourage students to experiment with projects on that topic.

Regardless of whether the subject of the book is mathematics or another topic that places math in context, the pictures are very important.

That is, the photos in *Great Estimations* will help students understand how to use each technique, just as the height-comparisons chart in *Skyscraper* (Curlee, 2007) can generate appropriate math problems. Teachers can capitalize on both kinds of books to create meaningful learning experiences.

Text sets can take the learning still further. Mr. DiSilva shared Curlee's (2007) picture book *Skyscraper* to help his math students make real-world connections. After the class did some percentage problems generated by the book, he distributed a number of nonfiction selections so students could find additional high-rise applications. He even included a poetry book, just for fun.

On the following pages, we present books of both kinds. Each was selected because it had the potential to generate a powerful understanding of mathematics and how it is used in the real world. Teachers of other subject areas are encouraged to look at the cross-curricular connections for each book to discover links to social studies, science, language arts, and the arts. (See Appendix A for a link to national math standards.)

Math is everywhere. Show students how true that statement really is by using some of these great picture books.

 ## The Mathematics of Bridges

Prince, April Jones, and François Roca. (2005). *Twenty-One Elephants and Still Standing.* Illustrated by François Roca. Boston: Houghton Mifflin. (FPB)

In 1883, fourteen years of work came to fruition when the Brooklyn Bridge was completed. April Jones Prince describes its beauty in lyrical prose: "woven steel cables, strung graceful and strong, like stairways straight to the stars" (unpaged). But despite the fact that the bridge was a wonder to behold, some people questioned whether such a lengthy span was safe. It seemed there always would be skeptics. To the rescue came circus mogul, P. T. Barnum. He arranged to take his circus to Brooklyn. Most of the attractions traveled by water, but the elephants walked straight down Broadway. And when they reached the bridge, they did not hesitate. Together, twenty-one elephants tested the integrity of the new bridge and showed that it was sound. Accompanied by François Roca's beautiful color illustrations, this fact-based story is a great way to interest students in the mathematics of bridges.

Activity Suggestions

1. ☻ *The strength of a triangle:* There are many kinds of bridges. Truss bridges use triangles to support the weight of the bridge. Challenge students

to experiment with different shapes cut from strips of cardboard to see for themselves if triangles are stronger than squares, rectangles, or octagons. Students also can find out whether there are different ways to align the triangles to increase the strength. Have students write a paragraph or draw a diagram to explain what they learned.

2. ☻ *It's a wrap:* Steel cables suspend the Brooklyn Bridge. These were made by bundling 278 steel wires together to make a "strand," then combining nineteen strands into a main cable. Each steel wire is about as thick as a pencil. Have students measure a pencil and calculate the approximate size of each main cable (15.75 inches in diameter). Ask students to create and solve an equation that would find the approximate thickness of each "strand."

3. ☻ or ☻☻ *Metric, please:* One expert estimates that each of the two huge bridge anchorages weighed 120,000 pounds. Ask students to write an equation to convert that weight into metric tons. To help students understand the concept of such a great weight, assign students to find out the weight of other, more familiar heavy objects (e.g., cars, elephants, etc.), convert those figures into metric tons as well, and calculate how many of the objects would equal the weight of the anchorages.

4. ☻☻ *A weighty subject:* In an author's note, April Jones Prince tells us that the average elephant weighs 10,000 pounds. Have students find out the approximate weight of a mid-size car. How many of these autos would equal the weight of Barnum's twenty-one elephants? Given the length of the Brooklyn Bridge (5,989 feet), is the fact that it can hold twenty-one elephants a true indication of safety for today's transportation needs? Why or why not? Have students find out how the bridge was changed to accommodate auto traffic. Extend this activity by asking small groups to research the lengths of specific bridges. Ask them to find out the weight of bumper-to-bumper traffic on each bridge. To make the project more challenging, stipulate that a given percentage of the traffic must consist of mid-size cars, SUVs, etc. (Students may find the weight and length of ANY vehicle that fits a specific category and use those statistics to represent all vehicles in that category, or you can agree as a class which models will be used.)

Cross-Curricular Connections

1. ☻ or ☻☻ *Social studies:* Create a "scavenger hunt" for your students. Display photographs of famous bridges and have small groups of students use the Internet to find out where they are/were and identify the type

of bridge construction. The time required will depend on the number of bridges they must find and the number of students in each group.

2. ☉☉ *Science:* Bridge designers must ask and answer many questions. Ask students to brainstorm such questions (e.g., what materials should be used to build the bridge? Will it carry cars or trains?). Online research will show students there are many variations on bridge designs. Have small groups create scale models of various designs. Specify the same length for all designs. Then, test the strength of each model using the same weights (e.g., coins). Which design seems to be the strongest?

3. ☉☉ *The arts:* Many bridges are beautiful. Ask your students to take photographs of local bridges and submit them for a "most beautiful bridge" contest. The whole class can generate judging criteria and then vote to select the winner.

Suggested Text Set for Mathematical Solutions

Adkins, Jan. (2002). *Bridges: From My Side to Yours*. Brookfield, CT: Roaring Brook Press. (NF)

Briscoe, Diana. (2005). *Bridge Building: Bridge Designs and How They Work*. Bloomington, MN: Red Brick Learning. (NF)

Curlee, Lynn. (2001). *Brooklyn Bridge*. New York: Atheneum for Young Readers. (NF)

Richards, Julie. (2004). *Bridges (Smart Structures)*. Illustrated by Margaret Hastie. North Mankato, MN: Smart Apple Media. (NF)

Scieszka, Jon, and Adam McCauley. (2002). *Hey Kid, Want to Buy a Bridge? (Time Warp Trio)*. Illustrated by Adam McCauley. New York: Viking. (FYA)

Weiner, Vicki. (2004). *The Brooklyn Bridge: New York City's Graceful Connection*. Architectural Wonders. New York: Children's Press. (NF)

 ### Making It Compute—Fibonacci Style

Hulme, Joy N., and Carol Schwartz. (2005). *Wild Fibonacci: Nature's Secret Code Revealed*. Illustrated by Carol Schwartz. Berkeley, CA: Tricycle Press. (NF/PB)

When Leonardo de Pisa published his book *Liber Abaci* in 1202, he shared a fascinating sequence of numbers. Writing under the pen name Fibonacci, he discovered the pattern known as the "Fibonacci sequence" with each number called a "Fibonacci number." What we know as the 1, 1, 2, 3, 5, 8, 13, 21, 34, and so on pattern (just add the two preceding numbers to get the next one) occurs in nature. Horns, claws, shells, even human teeth fit in the "equiangular spiral" plotted by Fibonacci. The book illustrations beautifully convey these patterns. The simple text draws any student into this most complex mathematical concept.

Activity Suggestions

1. ☺ or ☺☺ *The plot thickens:* Write a new sequence of numbers and have small groups work on writing a formula to find a specific element (e.g., the seventeenth number in the sequence). Discuss the resulting formulas and try them out to see if they work. On another day, students can create their own sequences. (For example: add three numbers, then two, then three, and so on.) Pairs of students could exchange sequences and see if they can discover the patterns, then try to write (and test) a formula for each one.

2. ☺ or ☺☺ *Fibonacci in my world:* On the last page, the author shares the Fibonacci numbers in her family (the author, 1 grandson, 2 grand-daughters, 3 great-granddaughters, and so on). Have the students explore their school building for the sequence and create a visual of the pattern (1 janitor, 1 principal, 2 cooks, 3 sixth-grade math teachers, etc.). Create large visuals that show the pattern, using drawings or symbols to represent the people or objects in their sequence. Post these in the hallway for other students and teachers to enjoy.

3. ☺ *Fibonacci rules:* The author explains that the dimensions of the book fit the Fibonacci pattern. Have students measure the book and test the proportions suggested. Are there other objects in the classroom to which they could apply this measurement? Have students suggest objects and then test their theory.

4. ☺ *Fibonacci and you:* The structure of the human body includes many examples of the Fibonacci sequence. Numerous websites give information about this. One of these sites is http://milan.milanovic.org/math/english/golden/golden2.html. View the website with the class. Challenge students to find the Fibonacci sequence as exhibited in the human hand. (The measurements are approximate for any given person, but the sequence fits across a larger population.)

Cross-Curricular Connections

1. ☺☺ *Language arts:* The book is written in rhyme. Have small groups of students compile a book with Fibonacci pattern rhymes using pictures they draw or cut from magazines (such as pinecones or seashells).

2. ☻☻ *Science:* Have students collect and bring in many plants to examine the Fibonacci sequence. These might include cauliflower, cucumbers, pears, apricots, geraniums, pussy willows, and pinecones. Use the illustrations in the book to guide their visual analysis of these objects.

3. ☻ *The arts:* Before Fibonacci published *Liber Abaci,* artists had long talked about the "golden triangle." Cut a "golden triangle" from a clear sheet of plastic. Make these of various sizes so students can select an appropriate one to work with. Have students lay the "golden triangle" on reproductions (or enlarged photographs of) paintings that demonstrate this shape. Discuss why this is pleasing to the eye.

Suggested Text Set for Mathematical Solutions

Bruno, Leonard C., and Lawrence W. Baker. (1999). *Math & Mathematicians: The History of Math Discoveries around the World.* Detroit, MI: U X L. (B)

Farndon, John. (2007). *Do Not Open: An Encyclopedia of the World's Best-Kept Secrets.* New York: DK Publishing. (NF)

Franco, Betsy, and Steve Jenkins. (2008). *Bees, Snails, & Peacock Tails: Patterns & Shapes . . . Naturally.* Illustrated by Steve Jenkins. New York: Margaret K. McElderry Books. (NF/PB)

McCallum, Ann, and Gideon Kendall. (2007). *Rabbits, Rabbits Everywhere: A Fibonacci Tale.* Illustrated by Gideon Kendall. Watertown, MA: Charlesbridge. (F/PB)

Patilla, Peter. (2000). *Patterns.* Portsmouth, NH: Heinemann Library. (NF)

Rau, Dana Meachen. (2002). *A Star in My Orange: Looking for Nature's Shapes.* Minneapolis, MN: Millbrook Press. (NF)

 Skyscrapers: High-Rise Math

Curlee, Lynn. (2007). *Skyscraper.* New York: Atheneum for Young Readers. (NF/PB)

The Great Pyramid at Giza, which rose 481 feet high, was the tallest manmade object in the world for almost 4,500 years. That record was shattered by the Washington Monument in 1885 (555 feet) and the Eiffel Tower in 1889 (986 feet). And after that, the sky was the limit. Lynn Curlee's book describes how this "uniquely American invention" (p. 2) appeared first in Chicago and New York City and then spread around the globe. In addition to a historical treatment, the author also discusses the technology that made skyscrapers possible and describes the work of various architects who made some of the world's most famous buildings a reality. Colorful illustrations with an art deco feel nicely complement the text.

A helpful comparison chart lets students see how each building stacks up to the competition. Here's a topic that provides plenty of context for mathematical thinking as students consider high-rise math.

Activity Suggestions

1. ☺ *Making comparisons:* Find out how big a skyscraper really is by comparing it to something students know well—their school building. Have students calculate the total volume of the school and the total volume of a specific skyscraper. How many schools would fit inside? If desired, this activity may be repeated with another skyscraper. (Note: if your "school" actually consists of multiple buildings, start with just one of them.)

2. ☺ or ☺☺ *That's quite a story:* Ask students to compare the height and the number of stories for each building in the book. Have them calculate the number of vertical feet allotted to each story. Is it the same for each building? How can they justify the different number of feet per story in various buildings? To extend this, specify the area for one story and the parameters for a typical office. How many such offices would fit on one story of the building? Estimate the floor area lost to elevators and stairwells on each floor. On a ten-story building, how much square footage is lost? On a twenty-story building?

3. ☺ or ☺☺ *Just a dream:* Frank Lloyd Wright designed a building that was meant to be a mile high (see comparison chart, p. 42). That building remains a "dream," but the author describes other new buildings that are challenging our notions of just how high mankind can build. Ask students to compare each skyscraper to a mile. What percent of a mile is each building's height? To extend this activity, have each student choose a building and compare it to something other than a mile (e.g., 1.7 times the height of the Statue of Liberty, 48 percent of the height of Mount Rushmore, etc.—it could be converted into metric units if desired). Note how the height of one building can be expressed in different ways.

4. ☺☺ *Let's build it:* Have students choose a skyscraper and create a scale model of it. (Discuss appropriate scales—e.g., would a model of a 1,000-foot building fit inside the classroom if students built it in a scale of one inch per foot?) Challenge them to be as accurate as possible. This project would work well for small groups.

Cross-Curricular Connections

1. ☺☺ *Social studies:* Ask students to consider the negative and positive consequences of modifying a city's environment to depend upon many

skyscrapers. With so many people working and/or living in these tall buildings, what issues arise regarding transportation, safety, health, etc.? Have students debate the pros and cons of this urban development.

2. ☻ *Science:* Have students investigate how an elevator works. Find out who invented it, when, and which simple machines contributed to its design. To understand the impact of this invention on the construction of skyscrapers, have students see how many continuous flights of stairs they can climb (or descend) without resting.

3. ☻ *The arts:* Share photographs of various skyscrapers. Ask students to critique them from an aesthetic standpoint. Discuss the meaning of the saying "form follows function" (Louis Sullivan; see p. 8). Which is more important to them, the form or the function? Why?

Suggested Text Set for Mathematical Solutions

Clements, Gillian. (2008). *The Picture History of Great Buildings*. London: Frances Lincoln Children's. (NF)

Gerstein, Mordicai. (2003). *The Man Who Walked between the Towers*. Brookfield, CT: Roaring Brook Press. (NF)

Hopkinson, Deborah, and James Ransome. (2006). *Sky Boys: How They Built the Empire State Building*. Illustrated by James Ransome. New York: Schwartz & Wade Books. (NF)

Janeczko, Paul B., and Robert Rayevsky. (2007). *Hey You! Poems to Skyscrapers, Mosquitoes, and Other Fun Things*. Illustrated by Robert Rayevsky. New York: HarperCollins. (P)

Kent, Peter. (2001). *Great Building Stories of the Past*. New York: Oxford University Press. (NF)

Mann, Elizabeth, and Alan Witschonke. (2003). *Empire State Building: When New York Reached for the Skies*. Wonders of the World Book. Illustrated by Alan Witschonke. Photographs by Lewis Hine. New York: Mikaya Press. (NF)

Zaunders, Bo, and Roxie Munro. (2004). *Gargoyles, Girders, and Glass Houses: Magnificent Master Builders*. Illustrated by Roxie Munro. New York: Dutton Children's Books. (NF)

 Great Estimations

Goldstone, Bruce. (2006). *Great Estimations*. New York: Henry Holt. (NF/PB)

Bright photos and interesting subjects are the focus of this book on estimation. An important skill in our current days of handheld calculators, the estimation practice provided on the pages of this book will help develop number sense. So, how many penguins are in the picture? Thirty or 30,000? Learning how to group the photographed items, students will see how to estimate a total number.

Activity Suggestions

1. ☺ or ☺☺ *Shopping excursion:* Provide grocery store ads to small groups of students. Give them a list of items to purchase and, using estimation, they must decide if $20 will buy what they need. Or, tell students they have only $20 to spend and have them estimate which of the items in the grocery store ad they could purchase without overspending. When they have completed both tasks, allow them to use calculators to see if they were correct. Have students figure out the percent of difference between their estimates and the actual numbers. As time allows, have them try again with $40 and/or $60. If desired, have the class make a comparison chart to show their results across all three attempts.

2. ☺ or ☺☺ *A penny's worth:* Weigh a roll of pennies. Have students feel the weight of the roll. Provide a checklist of classroom items the students should hold and estimate how many rolls of pennies are equivalent to each object's weight. After all estimations are completed, provide actual amounts. How close were they? To extend this activity, take an object that is worth X number of penny rolls and use that object to find other items of similar weight.

3. ☺ *Think outside the box:* The book features many pages of photographed items to estimate. Fill boxes with items and ask the students to estimate the total (Ping-Pong or golf balls, crayons, pinecones). Ask them what suggestions from the book they used to make their estimation and suggest others they could have used to be more accurate.

4. ☺ *Toothpick measurement:* Provide each student with a toothpick. Have them study the length. Then, using any number of measurable objects, have the students estimate how many toothpicks "long" each is. Select a range of objects, both easy and hard to use for "toothpick measurement" (pencil, book, wall chart, window, etc.). Which objects were easier to estimate? Why?

Cross-Curricular Connections

1. ☺ *Language arts:* Using one photo from the book, have students compose paragraphs that include precise language, sensory details, and colorful modifiers to describe. Compare the paragraphs in a large group.

2. 🕐 *Social studies:* Select maps that provide a scale of inches for miles. Discuss what the ratio provided (such as 1:5, for one inch equals five miles) means. Have students estimate mileages between cities, based on the scale provided.

3. 🕐 *Science:* Using images (from a textbook or the Internet), have students estimate the number of items in an enlargement of a microscopic slide and then how that "translates" into actual size. For instance, an enlargement of hair follicles may note how many hairs are on one square inch of the normal human head. Using that as a guide, have students estimate how many would be on a full head of hair. Similar estimating activities could be done with microscopic photos of bacterial cells, white blood cells versus red blood cells, pollen on plants, and water droplets on a window.

Suggested Text Set for Mathematical Solutions

Bauer, Joan. (1996). *Sticks*. New York: Delacorte Press. (FYA)

Clements, Andrew, and Mike Reed. (2006). *A Million Dots*. Illustrated by Mike Reed. New York: Simon and Schuster Books for Young Readers. (PB)

Goldstone, Bruce. (2008). *Greater Estimations*. New York: Henry Holt. (NF)

Schultz-Ferrell, Karren, Cathy Weiskopf, and Linda Powley. (2008). *Estimating and Measuring: Adventures in Mathopolis*. Hauppauge, NY: Barron's Educational Series. (FYA)

Schwartz, David M., and Marissa Moss. (1998). *G Is for Googol: A Math Alphabet Book*. Illustrated by Marissa Moss. Berkeley, CA: Tricycle Press. (ABC)

Sharp, Richard M., and Seymour Metzner. (1996). *The Sneaky Square and Other Math Activities for Kids*. Illustrated by Steve Hoeft. New York: TAB Books. (NF)

Mathematics of the Age of Chivalry

Firth, Rachel, Giancinto Gaudenzi, Lee Montgomery, Craig Taylor, Abigail Wheatley, Robert D. Smith, Jane Chisholm, and Jane Bingham. (2006). *Knights and Armor*. Illustrated by Giacinto Gaudenzi and Lee Montgomery. London: Usborne. (NF/PB)

Put math in context with this fascinating book on knights and armor. The book abounds with real-world applications of middle school math concepts. It is well organized, beginning with a table of contents and suggestions on how to use the many Internet links sprinkled throughout the book (clearly located in text boxes). Readers will enjoy learning about what knights did during peacetime or when they were at war. Detailed information about chivalry, famous battles, and a snapshot of what life was like in the Middle Ages are also presented. This highly attractive book features numerous color illustrations, diagrams, maps, and photographs that help to clarify the wealth of information included in the book. The text is formatted in short sections or paragraphs that improve readability for readers at various levels.

Activity Suggestions

1. ☺ *Medieval measurements:* In medieval times, units of measurement varied widely because they were developed locally. Help students understand this dilemma by asking them to pace off 100 "feet" (a "foot" being the length of each student's foot). Measure off 100 actual feet (in standard units) and have students compute the percentage of difference between their distance and the actual distance. Discuss the implications of nonstandard measurement units—e.g., for the length of a bridge, the height of a basketball hoop, etc.

2. ☺ *Target area:* Ask students to draw a diagram showing the area around a castle that must be protected from archers who could shoot an arrow up to 200 yards. Then, ask them to draw a similar model of the area to be protected from siege engines that could hurl an object twice that far. (They should use the same scale for each drawing.) Have them calculate the area in each case. What is the percentage increase in vulnerable territory when a siege engine is used? If the siege engine could be adjusted so it could hurl an object an additional fifty yards, what would be the percentage of increase in the area to be protected? Have students draw the model and calculate the area. Repeat with eighty yards, etc.

3. ☺ or ☺☺ *What a chore:* Knights wore suits of chain mail to protect them in battle. Collect rings from the tops of soft drink cans. Give each student twenty-five rings and ask them to connect the rings with wire or twist ties. Students record their time. Have them figure the average time for the class. According to the book, a chain-mail tunic was constructed of about 30,000 links. Using the class average time, how long would it take a student to make a tunic for one knight? For an army of sixty knights? If students could improve their time by 3 percent, how much time would that save? To extend this activity, have students interview modern-day workers to determine the time required for a specific task (e.g., changing a tire, frying a hamburger, etc.). Ask them to write problems about productivity and share them in class. Relate this to jobs, wages, etc. What is the impact of increased productivity?

4. ☼☼ *Think of the possibilities:* On pp. 48–49, Firth discusses the creation of coats of arms. Ask students to solve this problem: If there are four basic colors and two metallic colors, and a shield must have two or more colors, how many variations are possible? Have students sketch their own coats of arms at home. The next day, count the number of elements used and calculate the possible variations.

Cross-Curricular Connections

1. ☼ *Language arts:* This book includes a wealth of unfamiliar vocabulary. We learn that invaders sometimes dug tunnels beneath the castle walls to "undermine" them. This is related to the modern term meaning to injure someone in a deceitful manner. Ask students to look for additional words that are new to them. Can they find connections to other modern terms?

2. ☼ or ☼☼ *Social studies:* Find some medieval recipes. (The book includes a suggested link.) Compare the recipes to modern foods and methods of preparation. How has cooking changed throughout the ages? What dishes are no longer popular? Can any conclusions be drawn from the list of ingredients used? If possible, prepare one or more of the recipes and let students get a "taste" of medieval times.

3. ☼☼ *The arts:* Research racing silks worn by modern-day professional jockeys. Compare the variation found in coats of arms to the current design variation in racing silks. Discuss how they are the same or different. Ask students to create their own design for racing silks and explain the significance of each element.

Suggested Text Set for Mathematical Solutions

Adkins, Jan. (2006). *What If You Met a Knight?* New Milford, CT: Roaring Brook Press. (NF)

Byam, Michèle. (2004). *Arms and Armor.* DK Eyewitness Books. New York: DK. (NF)

Gravett, Christopher. (2008). *Knight: Noble Warrior of England, 1200–1600.* Oxford: Osprey. (NF)

Gurstelle, William. (2004). *The Art of the Catapult: Build Greek Ballistae, Roman Onagers, English Trebuchets, and More Ancient Artillery.* Chicago, IL: Chicago Review Press. (NF)

Hunt, Jonathan. (1989). *Illuminations.* New York: Bradbury Press. (ABC)

Neuschwander, Cindy, and Wayne Geehan. (2006). *Sir Cumference and the Isle of Immeter: A Math Adventure.* Illustrated by Wayne Geehan. Watertown, MA: Charlesbridge. (FPB)

Smith, Miranda, and Alex Pang. (2008). *Navigators: Knights and Castles.* Illustrated by Alex Pang. London: Kingfisher. (NF)

Math Every Day in Every Way

Lee, Cora, Virginia Gray, and Gillian O'Reilly. (2007). *The Great Number Rumble: A Story of Math in Surprising Places.* Illustrated by Virginia Gray. Toronto, ON: Annick Press. (FPB)

"What is math? The real question is: what isn't?" (p. 2). Thus we are drawn into this fast-paced, fun look at math. When the school director drops math from the curriculum (less stress for students, and they use calculators anyway!), Sam sets out to prove math is everywhere. Sam takes Mr. Lake on a tour of the school, showing how math fits in science, art, music, and more. Math aficionados, as well as those afraid of math, will enjoy the applications and explanations of everything from ratios to irrational numbers. The humor is sure to snag even the most reluctant reader or mathematician. Sam proves his theory, and along the way we learn a lot about math and famous mathematicians (Pythagoras, Archimedes, Hypatia of Alexandria, Sophie Germain, Charles Lutwidge Dodgson [yes, of *Alice in Wonderland* fame], and Andrew Wiles). Use of contemporary topics, such as movie digitizing, MP3 players, and magic tricks, makes this a fun and memorable book about math.

Activity Suggestions

1. ☺ *Where's the math?* Sam takes us on a journey of math every day and in every area of the curriculum. Have students expand the math focus in one of the areas. For instance, science shows that honeybee cells are hexagons. What other mathematical shapes are evident around us (think cones, cubes, etc.)? Relate the various shapes to the work of the famous mathematicians mentioned in the book.

2. ☺ *You say permutation, I say combination:* Sam shows how two pairs of pants, three shirts, and three pairs of boots can make eighteen different outfits. Have students create combinations (or permutations) using a number of items of personal interest (scoops of ice cream, songs on a favorite CD).

3. ☺☺ *Movie time:* Information is provided about the number of processors used and time needed to create 600,000 Orcs in *Lord of the Rings* (New Line Cinema, 2001, 2002, 2003). Have students research special effects for their favorite movies and find the mathematical connections this research provides.

4. ☻ *In your prime:* Sam provides a chart with prime numbers through 100. He claims no mathematician can find a pattern. First, examine the prime numbers from 1 to 100 to see what Sam was explaining. Then, have students complete the chart using numbers 100 to 200. How does this compare to the first chart? Why is it so hard to find a pattern after all?

Cross-Curricular Connections

1. ☻☻ *Language arts:* Many stories about mathematicians and the discoveries they made are shared in the book. Students could further explore biographies of a mathematician of interest or write short news articles announcing the mathematician's discovery using the 5W format (who, what, where, when, why). Suggest they craft an attention-getting headline for their article.

2. ☻ *Science:* Sam explains how ratios apply to bicycle gears. Bring in a bike to have students examine the gears and ratios. Use Sam's explanation to test the ratio information he provides. If possible, use bikes of different sizes (such as a youth size and an adult size). Are the ratios the same?

3. ☻☻ *The arts:* Sam shows how M. C. Escher applied mathematical principles to tessellations. Many of his drawings can be seen at his website, http://www.mcescher.com (along with interviews of M. C.). Have students study Escher's drawings and then have them create their own using any shape.

Suggested Text Set for Mathematical Solutions

Blum, Raymond, and Jeff Sinclair. (2001). *Mathemania*. Illustrated by Jeff Sinclair. New York: Sterling Publishing. (NF)

Demi. (1997). *One Grain of Rice: A Mathematical Folktale*. New York: Scholastic Press. (FT)

Ellis, Julie, and Phyllis Hornung Peacock. (2004). *What's Your Angle, Pythagoras? A Math Adventure*. Illustrated by Phyllis Hornung Peacock. Watertown, MA: Charlesbridge. (B)

Gow, Mary. (2005). *Archimedes: Mathematical Genius of the Ancient World*. Great Minds of Science. Berkeley Heights, NJ: Enslow Publishers. (B)

McKellar, Danica. (2007). *Math Doesn't Suck: How to Survive Middle School Math without Losing Your Mind or Breaking a Nail*. New York: Hudson Street Press. (NF)

Rallison, Janette. (2002). *Playing the Field*. New York: Walker & Co. (F)

Seymour, Dale, and Jill Britton. (1989). *Introduction to Tessellations*. Palo Alto, CA: Dale Seymour Publications. (NF)

Folding Math Applications into Paper Airplanes

Blackburn, Ken, and Jeff Lammers. (2006). *The World Record Paper Airplane Book*. Illustrated by David Allen. New York: Workman. (NF/PB)

Making paper airplanes is just a form of play, right? Wrong. With this book by Ken Blackburn and Jeff Lammers, it's also applied aeronautical engineering with many mathematical applications. Both authors are engineers: Lammers is a pilot, and Blackburn is the world record-holder for greatest time aloft for a paper airplane. Together, they have created a book that is filled with information and fun. Topics include drag and glide angle, ridge lift, and convections or thermals, to name a few. Black-and-white diagrams and illustrations clearly show how to create twenty different models, including the world record holder. Twenty ready-to-fold plane designs on stiff paper (and most with jazzy color graphics) complete the book. There's even a foldout "runway" for target practice. Who says learning can't be fun?

Activity Suggestions

1. ☼ *Take wing:* Have students choose and create one of the paper airplane designs in this book. Before flying their planes, ask them to estimate the surface area of the wings and record it. Then, do a "flight test" to compare the flights as to time and distance. Discuss which designs do better. Does the surface area appear to make a difference? What other variables could account for the difference in performance among the various designs?

2. ☼ *Make it bigger:* Ask students to predict what would happen to the surface area of their design's wings if they were to double the size of the paper used. Distribute the larger-sized paper and have students see if they were correct.

3. ☼ or ☼☼ *Center of attention:* Have each student fly his or her plane a specific number of times. Record the time aloft, the distance, or both on a class graph. To extend this activity, ask students to identify the mean, median, and mode for the class data sets. Note how extreme scores may have affected the mean. Ask students to predict what would happen if they increased the size of the data sets, then fly the planes again to collect more data and see if they were correct.

4. ☼☼ *Design your own:* Challenge students to create their own paper airplane designs. They should include step-by-step directions and diagrams (follow the examples in the book) and a record of time aloft and/or

distance for a specific number of trials. More able students could attempt a three-dimensional drawing of one or more views.

Cross-Curricular Connections

1. ☯ *Language arts:* John Gillespie Magee Jr.'s poem "High Flight" is considered by many to be the most famous poem about flight ever written. An American who joined the Royal Canadian Air Force to help fight Hitler's German army, Magee wrote this poem on the back of a letter to his parents. Read and discuss the poem. Consider the context—that Magee wrote it while flying at 30,000 feet. Ask students to evaluate the language used by the poet. Discuss why this poem is a fitting tribute to this pilot, who died at the age of nineteen, as well as to aviators everywhere. (Students may remember this poem quoted after Space Shuttle accidents. It may be found on numerous websites, including http://www.deltaweb.co.uk/spitfire/hiflight.htm).

2. ☯ *Science:* Flight is controlled by four basic forces: weight, lift, thrust, and drag. To show the importance of lift, demonstrate the experiment on p. 12 of Blackburn and Lammers' book. Create two identical paper planes and then crumple one into a ball. Throw them at the same level and speed. Students will see the crumpled ball hits the ground first because it has no lift (no wings). (Let student volunteers repeat with other designs to see if this always holds true.) Discuss why aircraft in space do not rely on lift. What powers their maneuvers? How do Newton's laws of motion come into play?

3. ☯ *The arts:* Read a version of the Greek myth about Daedalus and Icarus, who escaped an island prison on homemade wings. (See, for example, Warner's book in text set below.) Create and perform one or more scenes using story theater techniques (See Appendix B). Discuss pantomime techniques used by students.

Suggested Text Set for Mathematical Solutions

Carson, Mary Kay, and Laura D'Argo. (2003). *The Wright Brothers for Kids: How They Invented the Airplane, 21 Activities Exploring the Science and History of Flight.* Chicago: Chicago Review Press. (NF)

Grant, R. G. (2007). *Flight: 100 Years of Aviation.* New York: DK Publishing. (NF)

Jarrett, Philip. (2000). *Ultimate Aircraft.* New York: DK Publishing. (NF)

Masters, Nancy Robinson. (2004). *The Airplane.* Inventions that Shaped the World. New York: Franklin Watts. (NF)

Stillinger, Doug. (2004). *The Klutz Book of Paper Airplanes.* Palo Alto, CA: Klutz. (NF)

Yolen, Jane, and Jim Burke. (2003). *My Brothers' Flying Machine: Wilbur, Orville, and Me*. Illustrated by Jim Burke. Boston: Little, Brown. (B)

Warner, Rex. (2008). *Men and Gods: Myths and Legends of the Ancient Greeks*. Illustrated by Edward Gorey. New York: New York Review Books. (FT)

Go Figure!

Ball, Johnny. (2005). *Go Figure! A Totally Cool Book about Numbers*. New York: DK Publishing. (NF/PB)

This 95-page book could extend an entire year's math curriculum. Ball invites us into the world of math that is part of everything we do. He begins with a bit of history about numbers and how people around the world count. (Did you know the Babylonians gave us our sixty second/sixty minute standard? Or that the Faiwol tribe in Papua New Guinea uses twenty-seven body parts to count and name their numbers?) He moves onto the magical concepts of numbers around us, shapes, and finally the unusual places we might find math. This colorful and attractive book is packed with information, photographs, and interesting math challenges.

Activity Suggestions

1. ☻ *Zero is nothing?* Ball tells "a brief history of nothing" or the development of zero as a numeral (Aristotle said it should be illegal!). Using the brief stories he provides, expand the discussion of this topic. In particular, what role does zero play in the world around us? What other information can the students find about zero using the short stories Ball provides as a starting point?

2. ☻☻ *Standing on the shoulders of giants:* Isaac Newton gave us a memorable statement about his own genius. ("If I have seen farther, it was by standing on the shoulders of giants.") Humble words for such a gifted man. Ball offers a timeline of mathematicians and a short paragraph about each one's contribution to our understanding of mathematical concepts. Have students create a "who am I?" quiz game of the mathematician and his contribution (for example, "The word *algebra* comes from the title of a book I wrote." [Al Khwarizmi, 780–850 CE]). Add current-day mathematicians that they should know (Ball goes only as far as 1955 with Albert Einstein). To play the game, the student reads one clue at a time about his or her identity until someone in the class can guess who he or she is. (Make sure students structure clues related to mathematics and mathematical contributions.)

3. ☺☺ *Magic square of chess:* In his discussion of magic squares, Ball shows "A Knight's Tour" (p. 31). The Knight's Tour is a mathematical problem involving a knight on a chessboard. The knight is placed on the empty board and, moving according to the rules of chess, must visit each square exactly once (see http://threesixty360.wordpress.com/2008/09/16/the-math-of-chess). Use a chessboard (or simulate a board on an overhead projector) to demonstrate the moves shown in the book. If possible, have several chessboards so pairs of students can take turns trying the knight's tour. Then, have students create their own patterns using a knight on a chessboard (or have them use a different piece and create a different tour, such as a Bishop's Tour or the Castle Tour). Students record their moves on an 8 □ 8 square grid, drawing lines to show the path taken. This problem-solving activity ties in well with analytical thinking skills used in math. A lesson plan that teaches students about each game piece is available at http://www.lessonplanspage.com/MathChessProblemSolving28.htm.

4. ☺☺ *Magical math:* On pages 48 and 49, Ball shows the application of math in magic tricks. He provides a few examples, and students will no doubt want to try these. Most of the tricks challenge them to see the math concept without providing the answer. Have the students discover the concepts by working together to complete the trick and suggest what math concept it uses. Next, provide some magic trick books (see the following text set) and let students find others that rely on math concepts to "boggle" the minds of their classmates.

Cross-Curricular Connections

1. ☺ *Language arts:* Pages 8 and 9 show newspaper articles rewritten without numbers. So, the report about a high-jump athlete notes that he beat a previous record by "jumping a bit higher still" (p. 9). Ball shows how important numbers are in our everyday life. Have students use current newspaper articles or the school newsletter to rewrite articles. Students could select an article from the section of the paper they are most interested in: sports, current events, science/weather reports, and so on. They should rewrite an article, remove any numbers that appear, and replace the numbers with descriptive language. Which articles still made *some* sense and which ones were hard to understand no matter how descriptive the language? How much harder was it to convey the information in the article by using descriptive language instead of numbers?

2. ☺☺ *Social studies:* Cultural diversity abounds in this look at the origins of mathematical concepts and understandings. In particular, Ball shows

the development of numbers starting with the Babylonian system (and speculation that an oval might have represented a sack of wheat) to our current number system. Connect these discussions to current social studies topics. What was the significance of the letters used in Roman numerals (and why didn't they have zero)? What of the current-day Hadza tribe in Tanzania that only counts to three? What can we learn about their culture through their numbering system?

3. ☻ *The arts:* Have students find numerals in the local environment. You or the students could photograph the numbers and examine the stylistic differences. How does the style choice relate to the use of the number?

Suggested Text Set for Mathematical Solutions

Ho, Oliver, and Jeff Sinclair. (2001). *Amazing Math Magic*. Illustrated by Jeff Sinclair. New York: Sterling. (NF)

Lichtman, Wendy. (2007). *Do the Math: Secrets, Lies, and Algebra*. New York: Greenwillow Books. (FYA)

Maganzini, Christy, and Ruta Daugavietis. (1997). *Cool Math: Math Tricks, Amazing Math Activities, Cool Calculations, Awesome Math Factoids, and More*. Illustrated by Ruta Daugavietis. Los Angeles: Price Stern Sloan. (NF)

Pilegard, Virginia Walton, and Nicolas Debon. (2000). *The Warlord's Puzzle*. Illustrated by Nicolas Debon. Gretna. LA: Pelican. (PB)

Wingard-Nelson, Rebecca. (2004). *Data, Graphing, and Statistics*. Math Success. Berkeley Heights, NJ: Enslow Publishers. (NF)

Zaslavsky, Claudia. (2003). *More Math Games & Activities from around the World*. Chicago: Chicago Review Press. (NF)

Economics: Dollars and Cents

Hall, Alvin D. (2008). *Show Me the Money: How Money Affects You and Your World*. New York: DK Publishing. (NF/PB)

Economics need never be considered a dry topic. Renowned financial educator Alvin Hall cuts through all the complicated jargon of managing money and presents a book that will capture students' attention. Divided into four sections, the book includes topics such as *From Cows to Coins, The Cost of Living, The Global Economy*, and *How to Spend It*. Colorful graphic art on every page not only enhances understanding but also adds to the interest. Timelines, graphs, and text boxes add information, while a table of contents, glossary, and index make this a book that is easy to use.

Activity Suggestions

1. ☻ *The cost of not attending college:* Have students find out the cost of tuition for a local college. If they can complete a degree in four years, and the tuition does not increase, how much will the degree cost? Next, have students calculate how much they can make at a minimum wage job, working forty hours a week for one year. Then, compare that income to those listed on http://www.payscale.com for jobs that require a college degree. Ask students to calculate the percent of increase over the minimum wage job. Discuss the cost versus benefits of a college education.

2. ☻ or ☻☻ *Jackpot:* Students will enjoy the *Winner Takes All* topic (pp. 46–47), in which Hall shows alternate ways to claim and use a large cash prize. Put students in small groups and give each group a "winning lottery ticket" worth a different amount. Have them figure out how much a person would get if he or she took the lump sum (currently 28 percent for up to $164,550, 33 percent up to $357,700, and 35 percent above that). If the winner was 21 years old, how many years would he have to live to get more money by collecting $10,000 a year rather than taking the lump sum? Have each group choose the lump sum or graduated plan and outline how the winner could spend or invest the money. To extend this activity, groups can present (and justify) their plans.

3. ☻☻ *Cost of living:* To show students the cost of living on one's own, ask them to do some research. There are several possibilities. For example: (a) With a shopping list of specific items, students would comparison shop at two local grocery stores; (b) Students should ask parents to see a recent phone bill. Call the phone company to get prices and compare the cost of cellular versus landline service; (c) Ask students to do some "window shopping" at a used car lot. Find out the cost of a reliable used car and what the monthly payments would be. Add other research projects to fit students' needs and interests. Share information orally when research is completed.

4. ☻☻ *Teens just want to have fun:* Assign students to find the actual cost of going to their favorite entertainment (actual miles traveled from their home x lowest gas price they can find). Have them add that to the price of movie tickets, admission fee, etc., to find the total entertainment cost. Compare information in class the next day.

Cross-Curricular Connections

1. ☻☻ *Language arts:* Assign students to keep a "happiness" journal for one week. Each day they would write a paragraph about what made them

happiest. Then, at the end of the week, share the list Hall presents on pages 66–67 on eleven ways to be happier. Discuss whether students' choices matched the author's suggestions. Can they add anything to Hall's list?

2. ☉☉ *Social studies:* On pages 72–73, the author shows the many goods and services we use every day. To make this real for students, have them brainstorm a list of goods and services they use in a single day at school. Select specific resources and have students find out where they are produced. The next day, discuss the uneven distribution of productive resources in the world and how this affects the production of goods and services around the world.

3. ☉☉ *The arts:* Ask small groups of students to create board games that reflect their own community and the kinds of goods and services they consume. For a math connection, have students calculate the cost of their game (including hourly wage for those who created it). Share the games with other classes and ask them to vote on the best one. (Set standards for evaluation related to content, quality of workmanship, appearance, fun to play, etc.)

Suggested Text Set for Mathematical Solutions

Caes, Charles. J. (2000). *The Young Zillionaire's Guide to the Stock Market.* New York: Rosen. (NF)

Clements, Andrew, and Brian Selznick. (2007). *Lunch Money.* Illustrated by Brian Selznick. New York: Aladdin Paperbacks. (FYA)

Cribb, Joe. (2005). *Money.* New York: DK. (NF)

Orr, Tamra. (2009). *A Kid's Guide to Stock Market Investing.* Hockessin, DE: Mitchell Lane Publishers. (NF)

Paulsen, Gary. (2007). *Lawn Boy.* New York: Wendy Lamb Books. (FYA)

Reichblum, Charles. (2006). *What Happens to a Torn Dollar Bill? Dr. Knowledge Presents Facts, Figures, and Other Fascinating Information about Money.* New York: Black Dog & Leventhal. (NF)

Thomas, Keltie, and Stephen MacEachern. (2004). *The Kids Guide to Money Cent$.* Illustrated by Stephen MacEachern. Toronto, ON: Kids Can Press. (NF)

Probably Probability

Einhorn, Edward, and Adam Gustavson. (2008). *A Very Improbable Story.* Illustrated by Adam Gustavson. Watertown, MA: Charlesbridge. (FPB)

The probability of waking up with a talking cat on your head is something

Ethan never considered. But sure enough, Odds, a black cat full of probability challenges does just that. Ethan cannot get rid of Odds until he wins a probability game presented by the cat. He loses the coin jar draw (pennies and dimes), the sock drawer match (stripes and stars), and the marble bag challenge (four different colors). Ethan finally wins the cereal shape challenge, but then Odds suggests he apply the principle of probability to his upcoming soccer tournament. Using statistics from the last game, Ethan discovers his best shot for making a goal. Odds leaves as Ethan decides probability will probably make him a better soccer player today. This math adventure shows all the easy ways probability applies to everyday events and opens the door to many fun challenges students will enjoy.

Activity Suggestions

1. ☻ *Masters of probability:* At the end of the book, Einhorn provides a short history of probability. Have students research the actual challenge presented between French mathematicians Blaise Pascal and Pierre de Fermat in 1654 regarding a game of dice. Have sets of dice for students to replicate the challenge.

2. ☻ *Odds are:* Have students create their own probability challenges, similar to those Odds (the cat) gave to Ethan. What other situations in their house could create a challenge, or move the game to school (pencils in their desks, color of books on the library shelf, shoes in their locker). Have students pose the questions in written format and exchange with other students to solve.

3. ☻ *Be a sport:* Using past statistics from your school or local sports team, have students work out the probability of this year's wins. Based on previous years, which teams do they regularly beat, which do they regularly lose to? Are perceptions of "we always lose to . . . " correctly based on probability using past statistics?

4. ☻ *Weather the odds:* Meteorologists use probability to predict weather. Save a week's worth of newspapers. Use the prediction made on one day and the reported data on the next to decide how close the meteorologist was to the actual weather. Over a week, what is the probability that she or he will be right? If the meteorologist claimed there was a 50 percent chance of rain, what did that mean? What statistics does she or he use to make such a prediction?

Online Resources

Some wonderful interactive sites are available on the Web if you have access. Many allow the students to play a probability game online. Try these safe sites:

Spy guys: http://www.learnalberta.ca/Launch.aspx?content=%2fcontent%2fmesg%2fhtml%2fmath6web%2fmath6shell.html

Cyberchase: http://pbskids.org/cyberchase/games/probability

Cyberbee: http://www.cyberbee.com/probability/mathprob.html

National Center for Educational Statistics: http://nces.ed.gov/nceskids/chances

Mrs. Glosser's Math Goodies: http://www.mathgoodies.com/lessons/toc_vol6.html

BBC The Maths Files: http://www.bbc.co.uk/education/mathsfile/index.shtml

Cross-Curricular Connections

1. ☻☻ *Social studies:* Many games rely on probability to decide on moves. Games have historical roots that fit well with content studies of particular time periods. Have students research games, such as cribbage in the 1600s, solitaire in the 1700s, and Chinese checkers in the United States in the 1880s. (http://historicgames.com/gamestimeline.html provides a historic timeline of games.) How did the game develop over time?

2. ☻ *Science:* The author notes that probability is used in fields such as genetics. Have students chart the possible combinations of genes for such traits as eye color, hair color, attached or unattached earlobes, and so on.

3. ☻☻ *The arts:* Mozart played a dice game in which the results of throws would guide the choice between possible preselected bars of music. He would compose various bars of music and then roll the dice to determine which bar would be selected. He continued rolling and adding bars of music until he had a completed piece. Have students compose or select six short bars of musical notes. They can work together to create choices such as:

Each choice would be numbered 1 through 6. What is the probability of that bar being selected? Roll the die and compose the music. Small groups could work with the same six bars but roll their own die to see what composition they create.

Suggested Text Set for Mathematical Solutions

Anno, Mitsumasa, and Tsuyoshi Mori. (1986). *Socrates and the Three Little Pigs.* Illustrated by Mitsumasa Anno. New York: Philomel Books. (FPB)

Axelrod, Amy, and Sharon McGinley-Nally. (2000). *Pigs at Odds: Fun with Math and Games.* Illustrated by Sharon McGinley-Nally. New York: Simon & Schuster for Young Readers. (FPB)

Cushman, Jean, and Martha Weston. (2007). *Do You Wanna Bet? Your Chance to Find Out about Probability.* Illustrated by Martha Weston. New York: Clarion Books. (NF)

Leedy, Loreen. (2007). *It's Probably Penny.* New York: Henry Holt. (NF/PB)

Poskitt, Kjartan, and Philip Reeve. (2001). *Do you Feel Lucky? The Secrets of Probability.* Illustrated Philip Reeve. London: Hippo. (NF)

Roza, Greg. (2004). *Heads or Tails? Exploring Probability through Games.* Power-Math. New York: PowerKids Press. (NF)

Additional Cross-Curricular Connections

Find more math activities under these featured language arts books (Chapter 2):

Lucy Maud Montgomery: The Author of Anne of Green Gables (Wallner, 2006)

Louis Sockalexis: Native American Baseball Pioneer (Wise, 2007)

The Girl's Like Spaghetti: Why, You Can't Manage without Apostrophes! (Truss, 2007)

You Let the Cat Out of the Bag! (And Other Crazy Animal Sayings (Klingel, 2008)

Sugar Cane: A Caribbean Rapunzel (Storace, 2007)

My Librarian Is a Camel: How Books Are Brought to Children around the World (Ruurs, 2005)

One Million Things: A Visual Encyclopedia (Bryan, 2008)

The Titanic: An Interactive History Adventure (Temple, 2008)

Find more math activities under these featured social studies books (Chapter 3):

Yatandou (Whelan, 2007)

The Brothers' War: Civil War Voices in Verse (Lewis, 2007)

The Many Rides of Paul Revere (Giblin, 2007)

Dear Mr. Rosenwald (Waterford, 2006)

Muhammad (Demi, 2003)

Ain't Nothing but a Man: My Quest to Find the Real John Henry (Nelson & Aronson, 2008)

Lady Liberty: A Biography (Rappaport, 2008)

One Well: The Story of Water on Earth (Strauss, 2007)

Find more math activities under these featured science books (Chapter 5):

The Leaping, Sliding, Sprinting, Riding Science Book: 50 Super Sports Science Activities (Mercer, 2006)

Cave Detectives (Harrison, 2007)

The Down-to-Earth Guide to Global Warming (David & Gordon, 2007)

Amazing Leonardo da Vinci Inventions You Can Build Yourself (Anderson, 2006)

Ouch! How Your Body Makes It through a Very Bad Day (Walker, 2007)

Cool Stuff 2.0 and How It Works (Woodford & Woodcock, 2007)

The Story of Salt (Kurlansky, 2006)

Find more math activities under these featured arts books (Chapter 6):

How Does the Show Go on? An Introduction to the Theater (Schumacher & Kurtti, 2007)

Kamishibai Man (Say, 2005)

Archie's War: My Scrapbook of the First World War (Williams, 2007)

The Pot That Juan Built (Andrews-Goebel, 2002)

Paper, Scissors, Sculpt! Creating Cut-and-Fold Animals (Gonzales, 2005)

What's the Big Idea? Activities and Adventures in Abstract Art (Raimondo, 2008)

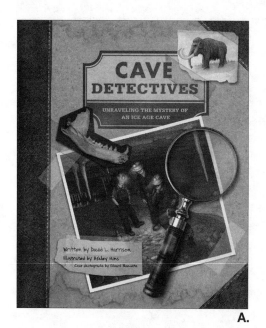

A.

B.

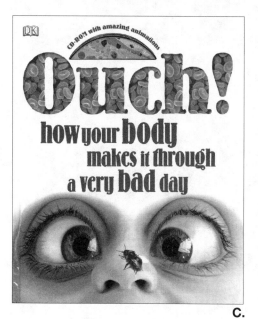

C.

D.

A. *Cave Detectives: Unraveling the Mystery of an Ice Age Cave* by David L. Harrison; illustrated by Ashley Mims. **B.** *Into the Volcano* by Donna O'Meara. **C.** *Ouch! How Your Body Makes It through a Very Bad Day* by Richard Walker. **D.** *Team Moon: How 400,000 People Landed Apollo 11 on the Moon* by Catherine Thimmesh.

5 Discovering through Picture Books in Science

[Science is] an imaginative adventure of the mind seeking truth in a world of mystery.

—Sir Cyril Norman Hinshelwood

cience. The very word conjures up an image of chemicals mixed in small glass tubes, beakers filled with bubbling liquids, and maybe even an unexpected puff of smoke. Somehow we *know* science is a subject in which exciting things should be happening.

In science class, students can unleash the sense of wonder that all but disappears at the end of the primary grades. Students who are "too cool" to be engaged in learning may find that science is one subject that is not the same old thing. It is the class where all modalities are put to work on a daily basis as students tackle hands-on/minds-on tasks. Science class is a place for hypotheses to be generated, checked, and (sometimes) confirmed. Science class is a place for discoveries!

Picture books can help to facilitate those discoveries. Sharing a well-crafted picture book is a great way to generate interest in a new topic. Want to get students hooked on the study of outer space? Read some quotes from *Team Moon: How 400,000 People Landed Apollo 11 on the Moon* (Thimmesh, 2006). Need an intriguing way to generate interest in inventors and inventions? Immerse students in building some of the most creative inventions of all time with Maxine Anderson's (2006) *Amazing Leonardo da Vinci Inventions You Can Build Yourself.*

Though most of students' discoveries will be made in the lab, picture books can extend what they are learning in class. For example, after students have spent time examining rocks of all kinds, they can read *The Story of Salt* (Kurlansky, 2006) for a look at one rock that is unique in many ways. Or, if you've been studying global warming, *The Down-to-Earth Guide to Global Warming* (David & Gordon, 2007) will offer plenty of additional information to build on what students have learned.

Picture books can also send students in completely new directions. *Ouch! How Your Body Makes It through a Very Bad Day* (Walker, 2007) can inject excitement into health-related topics. And students will realize that science is everywhere after reading Bobby Mercer's (2006) fun treatment of sports science, *The Leaping, Sliding, Sprinting, Riding Science Book: 50 Super Sports Science Activities.*

Text sets let teachers tap into students' interests. For example, when a television program sparked questions in Ms. Faraday's science classroom, she turned to the picture book *Solving Crimes with Trace Evidence* (Jeffrey, 2008). Interest was so high that she extended classroom activities with nonfiction and biography selections to encourage further research.

As always, the pictures do make a big difference. The best illustrations extend the text and reflect its mood. Thus, amazing black-and-white or color photos make a moon landing come alive or highlight the dangerous beauty of an erupting volcano, while humorous, cartoon-like illustrations emphasize the fun of sports science.

This chapter presents books that address a range of science topics. These are books that support students' interest in the world around them. Not only do they provide some of the answers to students' questions, but they also inspire additional research. Teachers of other content areas will find connections to their subjects as well. (See Appendix A for a link to national science standards.)

Science is all about discovery. Use these great picture books to enhance the joy of discovery in your own classroom.

Forensics: Science Applied to Solving Crimes

Jeffrey, Gary, and Peter Richardson. (2008). *Solving Crimes with Trace Evidence.*
    Graphic Forensic Science. Illustrated by Peter Richardson. New York:
    Rosen Central. (NF/PB)

This book makes a great springboard to addressing scientific inquiry and scientific ways of knowing. Part of the Graphic Forensic Science series, Jeffrey's book combines information presented in typical nonfiction format with famous cases written as graphic novels. Share book sections on fingerprints, microscopic evidence, DNA, and the like, and then ask students to read one of the three graphic inserts on their own. Each insert showcases how evidence was collected and used to convict a criminal. Reluctant readers will appreciate the graphic-novel format. Full-color photos and graphics add interest, while a glossary, list of references, and an index increase the book's usefulness.

Activity Suggestions

1. ☻ *Innocent until proven guilty:* This topic has strong ties to scientific ethics. What is the impact of bias in the examination and interpretation of trace evidence? Because forensic scientists often testify at trials, they must be able to accurately describe what they have found. Sometimes they also

must interpret the evidence. What is the difference? Watch a film clip from a TV courtroom drama. Ask students to explain how they know whether the forensic expert is providing description or interpretation.

2. ☻ *Trying out forensic sciences:* Students can "try out" some forensic tasks. For example, they can examine various human hairs under a microscope and compare them with animal hairs. How do they differ? Then, have students use the microscope to study the structure of birds' feathers, various kinds of soil or plants, carpet fibers, etc. After studying the evidence, how do scientists identify it?

3. ☻ or ☻☻ *No two alike:* Give students ink pads to take their thumbprints. Have them identify the characteristic arches, whorls, and loops that are used to categorize fingerprints. Then, have them compare their thumbprints with those of other students to see how each person's are unique. Graph the number of students whose prints exhibit arches, whorls, and loops. Assign students to find out the percentage of people who typically have arches, whorls, or loops. How closely does the class match that pattern? To extend this activity, enlarge the data set by having students collect fingerprints from students outside the class. Again, compare the results to what would be expected in the general population. Discuss how enlarging the research population can affect results.

4. ☻☻ *Tools of the trade:* Visit a police lab to see forensic scientists in action. Find out what kinds of tools they use to do their job. Discuss the safety procedures that are implemented to protect workers from infectious diseases. Find out what legal procedures protect the evidence from contamination.

Cross-Curricular Connections

1. ☻☻ *Language arts:* In criminal investigations, separating fact from opinion becomes very important. Have students observe some event (either live or on film) and write careful descriptions that include facts only. Let small groups of students share and compare what they have written and discuss which elements should be included or omitted. Then, have students rewrite their descriptions to omit any opinions.

2. ☻ *Social studies:* To test students' views toward people of other cultures, show them a "lineup" of photographs ("mug shots") and ask them to choose the criminal. The Federal Bureau of Investigation (FBI) site has photos of criminals. Use other photos of unknown people of various cultures. Discuss their choices and then share the identity of the true criminal.

3. ☺ or ☺☺ *The arts:* Police sketch artists help solve crimes or find missing persons by using a person's verbal description to draw a likeness of another individual. With the class, study the various shapes of eyes, noses, ears, etc. Then, verbally describe an individual while the students take the role of "sketch artist." Ask students to be as accurate as possible. Have a photo of the individual handy to let students check the accuracy of their portraits. As a follow-up, let students draw one another so they can see how much easier it is to create a portrait of someone they can see. Discuss how well they have captured their subjects. Ask them to speculate on the differences between the kinds of portraits drawn by a police artist and those commissioned by the subject.

Suggested Text Set for Further Discoveries

Cooper, Christopher. (2008). *Forensic Science.* New York: DK Publishing. (NF)

Denega, Danielle. (2007). *Have You Seen This Face? The Work of Forensic Artists.* 24/7, Science behind the Scenes. New York: Franklin Watts. (NF)

Hopping, Lorraine Jean. (2005). *Bone Detective: The Story of Forensic Anthropologist Diane France.* Women's Adventures in Science. New York: Franklin Watts. (B)

Jones, Charlotte Foltz, and David G. Klein. (1999). *Fingerprints and Talking Bones: How Real-Life Crimes Are Solved.* New York: Bantam Doubleday Dell Books for Young Readers. (NF)

Platt, Richard. (2005). *Forensics.* Kingfisher Knowledge. London: Kingfisher. (NF)

Walker, Richard. (2003). *Genes and DNA.* London: Kingfisher. (NF)

 ## To the Moon: A Perilous Journey

Thimmesh, Catherine. (2006). *Team Moon: How 400,000 People Landed Apollo 11 on the Moon.* Boston: Houghton Mifflin. (NF/PB)

This marvelous book details what went on behind the scenes before, during, and after that historic moment in 1969 when Neil Armstrong took man's first step on the surface of the moon. Most people know there were three astronauts involved, but the book's title lets us know there were many, many people who served on the support team. Students will be amazed to read about the range of tasks done by 400,000 others—engineers and seamstresses, flight directors and suit testers, to name just a few. The author's liberal use of direct quotes adds to the authenticity of the text and boosts interest for the reader. Virtually every page is filled with amazing photos, most of them taken from NASA archives. The majority of them are in color. Paired with white text on a black page, they are evocative of the moon shining in a night sky.

Activity Suggestions

1. ☻ *Speaking the language:* This book introduces students to vocabulary that is very specific to the topic. Have them create a glossary of terms (and acronyms) that will help them understand this book. Challenge them to find other space-related words that are not used in the book and expand the glossary to include them as well.

2. ☻ *Moon walk:* Allow students to see a video of the July 21, 1969, walk on the moon (currently available on YouTube) and point out the effects of the moon's gravity on the astronauts' movements. Have the students calculate their weight on the moon and other planets based on information about gravity on each one.

3. ☻ *Are we there yet?* The moon and the planets are very far from our earth. Compare those distances to the much greater distances man would have to travel to reach even the nearest stars. This is a good time to talk about light years (the distance light travels in one year, or 5,865,696,000,000 miles per year). Have students research the distance to a given star and then calculate how long it would take to reach it with our current technology.

4. ☻☻ *Technology connections:* When reading or hearing the book, students may find it fascinating to read passages like this: "Bob Nance, backroom support for CONTROL, was calculating the seconds of fuel remaining on his paper strip chart" (p. 27). Ask them to be alert for tasks that were done by hand/on paper that currently are done by computers. What was the role of the computer in 1969? What tasks have been taken over by computers for current-day space shuttle launches? To extend this activity, have small groups select a career of interest and research the technological changes in that field. On another day, ask the groups to share what they have learned. What conclusions can they draw?

Cross-Curricular Connections

1. ☻ *Language arts:* Most planets' natural satellites have names. However, our moon is simply referred to as the moon. Have students participate in a "Name that Moon" contest. They must come up with a name and write a persuasive essay about how the name was chosen and why it should be selected.

2. ☻ *Social studies:* Many jobs are necessary to bring a product or a project to successful completion. Have small groups of students select a specific product (e.g., chocolate chip cookies) and list all the jobs that must be

done to bring that product to the shelf. Individual students can research specific jobs. A more challenging task would be for them to select a complex project like landing on the moon (or organizing relief efforts after a natural disaster).

3. ☺☺ *The arts:* Students are probably familiar with paintings called "landscapes." One former lunar astronaut, Alan Bean, became a painter in later life. His "moonscapes" offer a unique perspective on the landscape of the moon. Find his work online for students to view (available on various websites; for example, http://www.novaspace.com/AUTO/ABorig/ABorig.html). Ask them to try painting a landscape of a scene they can view and then paint one after seeing a photo only. Discuss which is easier. Why? How does it help the artist to actually see what he or she is painting? Why is Alan Bean uniquely qualified to paint landscapes of the lunar surface?

Suggested Text Set for Further Discoveries

Barnett, Alex. (2004). *Space (DK Revealed)*. New York: DK Publishing. (NF)

Bingham, Caroline. (2008). *First Space Encyclopedia*. New York: DK Publishing. (NF)

Florian, Douglas. (2007). *Comets, Stars, the Moon, and Mars: Space Poems and Paintings*. Orlando, FL: Harcourt. (P)

Graham, Ian. (2004). *Space Travel*. E.guides. New York: DK Publishing. (NF)

Holden, Henry M. (2004). *Trailblazing Astronaut John Glenn*. Space Flight Adventures and Disasters. Berkeley Heights, NJ: MyReportLinks.com Books. (B)

Tocci, Salvatore. (2002). *Space Experiments*. A True Book. New York: Children's Press. (NF)

 ## Science Applied in Sports

Mercer, Bobby, and Tom LaBaff. (2006). *The Leaping, Sliding, Sprinting, Riding Science Book: 50 Super Sports Science Activities*. Illustrated by Tom LaBaff. New York: Lark Books. (NF/PB)

What helps a tennis player put topspin on a tennis ball? Why does a curve ball curve, and why is a "spit ball" hard to hit? What advantage do short people have when playing sports? These are just a few of the questions answered in this book by Bobby Mercer. In a conversational tone, Mercer provides step-by-step directions for dozens of easy experiments that allow the reader to discover the science behind a range of sports. A following section titled "What's Going On?" explains the science principles involved and presents necessary terminology in bold type. A table of contents and glossary help students find the information they need. Humorous color illustrations by Tom LaBaff show both male and female athletes competing. This is a book that will make science fun.

Activity Suggestions

1. ☻ *The thrill of victory:* The Olympics offers a range of sports many Americans do not otherwise see. Watch a video of an Olympic event. Challenge students to pinpoint the role science can play in winning and losing. Students should take notes and compare them afterwards.

2. ☻☻ *Tennis anyone?* Assign specific sports to small groups. Ask each group to explore the related science principles by performing two or more experiments from this book. Presentations on the following day will allow students to compare the science of various sports.

3. ☻☻ *Field trip:* Attend a basketball, baseball, or football game. Ask students to list examples of applied science they see. Follow up during the next class period with a discussion of what they saw. Have students (small groups or individuals) create posters demonstrating where kinetic and/or potential energy was evident in the events of the game.

4. ☻☻ *Find it:* After students are familiar with the various principles explained in this book, create a TV scavenger hunt by assigning specific concepts (e.g., force, acceleration, speed, momentum, friction, etc.) and having students watch sports to find examples in action.

Cross-Curricular Connections

1. ☻☻ *Language arts:* Sports are full of action, so this is a great topic to inspire the use of action words. Create lists of synonyms and have students use them to write appropriate paragraphs about sports events. For example, does a player always "run"? Might he or she sometimes "dash" or "jog" or even "lope"? Let students experiment with choosing more precise words for their writing. On another day, have them share their paragraphs by reading them aloud. Extend this activity by pulling quotes from stories students have read. Ask them to evaluate whether the author chose the most precise verbs.

2. ☻ *Mathematics:* Help students understand the importance of precise time in sports by watching a film clip of an Olympic race (track, skiing, etc.). Note the tiny gradations of time between first, second, and third place winners. Have students figure the percentage difference between gold, silver, and bronze medalists' times.

3. ☺☺ *The arts:* Explore the work of sports artists like James Fiorentino, Ernie Barnes, and others. Challenge students to put action on paper in a drawing or painting of their favorite sport.

Suggested Text Set for Further Discoveries

Goodstein, Madeline P. (1999). *Sports Science Projects: The Physics of Balls in Motion.* Science Fair Success. Berkeley Heights, NJ: Enslow Publishers. (NF)

Hammond, Tim, and Dave King. (2005). *Sports.* DK Eyewitness Books. New York: DK Publishing. (NF)

Herzog, Brad, and Mark Braught. (2004). *T Is for Touchdown: A Football Alphabet.* Illustrated by Mark Braught. Chelsea, MI: Sleeping Bear Press. (ABC)

Herzog, Brad, and Melanie Rose. (2004). *H Is for Home Run: A Baseball Alphabet.* Illustrated by Melanie Rose. Chelsea, MI: Sleeping Bear Press. (ABC)

Prelutsky, Jack, and Christopher Raschka. (2007). *Good Sports: Rhymes about Running, Jumping, Throwing, and More.* Illustrated by Christopher Raschka. New York: Alfred A. Knopf. (P)

Sylvester, Kevin. (2005). *Sports Hall of Fame, Weird.* Toronto, ON: Kids Can Press. (NF)

 ### Unraveling Ice Age Mysteries

Harrison, David L. (2007). *Cave Detectives: Unraveling the Mystery of an Ice Age Cave.* Illustrated by Ashley Mims. Cave photographs by Edward Biamonte. San Francisco, CA: Chronicle Books. (NF/PB)

Excavation for a new road in Springfield, Missouri, presented a big surprise for the construction company. When the road crew set off the explosives to remove part of a hill in the way, the earth collapsed rather than shoot thirty feet in the air. This told the construction crew that they better have a closer look. What they found was an ice age cave that had been sealed off for millions of years. Soon, scientists from a range of fields (geology, paleontology, hydrology) come to Riverbluff Cave to begin their research. Harrison unravels for us many of the mysteries presented by what the scientists found. Because the cave was sealed, footprints of peccary look fresh, claw prints on the walls from short-faced bears and saber-tooth cats (or American cats) can easily be seen and identified. A fossil found in a lower chamber may be an unknown centipede or millipede. The book contains plenty of unsolved mysteries to investigate. Accompanied by photos, drawings, and notebook paper "notes," this book is sure to capture the interest and imagination of students.

Activity Suggestions

1. ☺☺ *Calling all scientists:* The cave discovery crossed a number of science fields. Have students investigate and report on the jobs of each member of the research team involved in examining this discovery. These include geologists, paleontologists, hydrologists, and scientists who do carbon dating.

2. ☺ *Science first, building second:* The discovery in the cave halted the building of a road. Lead your class on a virtual field trip via one of the links at http://www.mnsu.edu/emuseum/archaeology/virtual/links.html.

3. ☺ *Rock identification:* The book shows many photographs and explains the many layers of earth and rock that were discovered in the cave. Photographs show stalactites and stalagmites. Have students examine the photos and make note of how calcite, limestone, and quartz differ. If you have rock samples available, have the students compare them to the photographs and descriptions given in the book.

4. ☺ *Just how old are you?* The ability to carbon-date can give an approximate date of fossils such as those found at Riverbluff. But, Harrison claims, the dating can be millions of years off. Have students research what is entailed in radiocarbon dating. How is it done? What is the scientific process? Why can there be such a range in "age" provided by the dating?

Cross-Curricular Connections

1. ☺ *Language arts:* Create an anticipation guide (See Appendix B). Have students respond to statements about caves before hearing or reading this book. Constructing sentences that probe for ideas they have that might not be true (e.g., "bats like to get in people's hair") is a good way to assess their prior knowledge.

2. ☺ *Social studies:* David Harrison provides examples of other states having similar caves (Tennessee, Texas, Missouri, and Virginia). Have students find the locations of these. Using a large United States map, have students place pins where these caves are. Is there any pattern to the locations? Have they ever visited any of these caves in other states? If so, have them share their experiences.

3. ☺ *Mathematics:* Radiocarbon dating provides an opportunity for students to construct interesting mathematical problems. Using the information gathered about how dating is done, create word problems that students can exchange and solve. Both the text and time line at the back of the book provide lots of opportunities for solving math problems.

Suggested Text Set for Further Discoveries

Berkowitz, Jacob, and Steve Mack. (2006). *Jurassic Poop: What Dinosaurs (and Others) Left Behind*. Illustrated by Steve Mack. Tonawanda, NY: Kids Can Press. (NF)

Jenkins, Steve. (2005). *Prehistoric Actual Size*. Boston: Houghton Mifflin. (NF)

Kerley, Barbara, and Brian Selznick. (2001). *The Dinosaurs of Waterhouse Hawkins: An Illuminating History of Mr. Waterhouse Hawkins, Artist and Lecturer*. Drawings by Brian Selznick. New York: Scholastic. (NF)

Larson, Peter L., and Kristin Donnan. (2004). *Bones Rock! Everything You Need to Know to Be a Paleontologist*. Montpelier, VT: Invisible Cities Press. (NF)

Lindop, Laurie. (2006). *Cave Sleuths*. Minneapolis: Twenty-First Century Books. (NF)

Morrison, Taylor. (2001). *The Great Unknown*. Boston: Houghton Mifflin. (B)

Sheldon, David. (2006). *Barnum Brown: Dinosaur Hunter*. New York: Walker & Co. (B)

 ## Global Warming: Ice Age Warning?

David, Laurie, and Cambria Gordon. (2007). *The Down-to-Earth Guide to Global Warming*. Illustrated by Stephen Schudlich. New York: Scholastic. (NF/PB)

Laurie David, producer of the Academy Award-winning film *An Inconvenient Truth,* and children's book author Cambria Gordon have created this attractive and intriguing book on global warming. They make a case for the reality of global warming and relate it to things that are important to middle school students (for example, lack of snow that might close skiing and snowboarding venues.) The reader-friendly text is written with a sense of humor that will appeal to students, and readers at all levels can handle the short topical sections (usually two to four pages). Numerous color photographs, illustrations, graphs, maps, and text boxes enhance both interest and comprehension. This book appeals to the middle schooler's desire to make the world a better place.

Activity Suggestions

1. ☻ *Storm season:* The authors claim global warming increases the strength of hurricanes. Assign each student a year (go back as far as necessary to involve the whole class) and have them find out the number of hurricanes and their intensity. Then, come back together for a whole-group discussion. Does their data support the authors' claim or refute it?

2. ☻ *Check it out:* Bring in sample tree rings, each labeled as to its location and the year when the tree was planted. Let students study the tree rings and draw conclusions about the impact of global warming based on information in the book. Students should be prepared to defend their conclusions.

3. ☻☻ *Become a "tree hugger":* According to the book (p. 15), one tree can absorb the amount of carbon dioxide released by an average car that was driven 4,000 miles. Ask students to total the number of miles driven on all the cars in their household (check the odometers). Then have them calculate how many full-size trees would be needed to absorb that much carbon dioxide. The results should make for a lively discussion.

4. ☻☻ *Take sides:* Students should learn that, like most issues, the idea of global warming is not universally embraced. Ask students to do Internet research to see what the "other side" has to say. Challenge students to choose one position and create a poster to defend it.

Cross-Curricular Connections

1. ☻ or ☻☻ *Language arts:* This issue presents the perfect opportunity for students to write persuasive letters. For example, they can write to members of congress urging the passage of an earth-friendly bill, to local authorities requesting recycling measures be put in place, or to a corporation praising or complaining about its policies. Send the letters and let students experience social action. (The amount of time required will depend on whether or how much the students must research before writing the letters.)

2. ☻☻ *Mathematics:* On p. 75, the authors suggest having each student swap one regular light bulb for a compact fluorescent bulb. Find out the cost differential between one standard 60-watt bulb and a 15-watt compact fluorescent bulb. Have students figure out how much more it would cost to install the compact fluorescent bulbs in their homes (each student has to count the number of bulbs in his or her house). Then, have them adjust for efficiency (i.e., if a fluorescent bulb lasts X times longer, the cost of the standard bulbs would be multiplied by X). See which kind of bulb is really more expensive. Discuss their findings and have them justify their positions.

3. ☻ *The arts:* Because global warming is an issue on which there is no one expert opinion, students can benefit from doing some role playing (see Appendix B). You can write the scenarios or ask your students to write

them. Divide the class into small groups of about three or four students. Give each group one scenario and allow a short time for them to prepare (e.g., five to ten minutes). Then, let groups present their role plays. Open the floor for discussion of the presentations —both as to content and acting techniques.

Suggested Text Set for Further Discoveries

Albert, Toni, and Margaret Brandt. (2000). *I Heard the Willow Weep.* Illustrated by Margaret Brandt. Mechanicsburg, PA: Trickle Creek Books. (P)

Cherry, Lynne, and Gary Braasch. (2008). *How We Know What We Know about Our Changing Climate: Scientists and Kids Explore Global Warming.* Nevada City, CA: Dawn. (NF)

Hall, Julie, and Sarah Lane. (2007). *A Hot Planet Needs Cool Kids: Understanding Climate Change and What You Can Do About It.* Illustrated by Sarah Lane. Bainbridge Island, WA: Green Goat Books. (NF)

Lasky, Kathryn, and Stanley Fellows. (2006). *John Muir: America's First Environmentalist.* Illustrated by Stanley Fellows. Cambridge, MA: Candlewick Press. (B)

Rhatigan, Joe, and Heather Smith. (2001). *Sure-to-Win Science Fair Projects.* Illustrated by Orrin Lundgren. New York: Lark Books. (NF)

VanCleave, Janice Pratt. (2004). *Janice VanCleave's Science around the World: Activities on Biomes from Pole to Pole.* Hoboken, NJ: John Wiley & Sons. (NF)

 ## Inventions: The Genius of Leonardo da Vinci

Anderson, Maxine. (2006). *Amazing Leonardo da Vinci Inventions You Can Build Yourself.* Norwich, VT: Nomad Press. (NF/PB)

Involve tactile learners in science by using *Amazing Leonardo da Vinci Inventions You Can Build Yourself* by Maxine Anderson. Following an introductory section about the Renaissance and Leonardo da Vinci's life, the material is divided into five chapters. Each chapter includes contextual information and specific instructions for making several of da Vinci's inventions. The author lists necessary materials and provides plenty of detailed diagrams that will help students follow the directions more easily and accurately. Students can make a camera obscura, a hygrometer, an ornithopter, and more. To increase learning possibilities, the author includes important information in text boxes. The book ends with a glossary, a list of print and web-based resources, and an index. Students who like the "hands-on" approach to education will love this book.

Activity Suggestions

1. ☽ *The modern version:* Using the directions in the book, have students make Leonardo's monkey wrench and then compare it to a modern-day version of the same tool. Test both to see which works better. Discuss adaptations that have been made to increase the efficiency of the wrenches we have today.

2. ☽ *See how it works:* One of the more unusual of da Vinci's inventions was his "walk-on-water shoes" (p. 69). This invention can be seen in action in the movie *Ever After* (Fox, 1998). A film clip of only a few minutes should pique students' interest. Compare what they see in the movie to the diagram in the book. Ask if they think the author's interpretation agrees with that of the movie producers. Challenge interested students to try making their own walk-on-water shoes and test them in shallow water.

3. ☽☽ *Getting from here to there:* For a fun project, have students construct a model of Leonardo's portable "safety bridge" (p. 100). Test it outdoors to evaluate its usefulness.

4. ☽☽ *Ideas versus reality:* Many of Leonardo's inventions never got past the drawing board stage in his lifetime. Ask students to find out via the Internet when these creative ideas finally became a reality and who gets credit for the invention. On another day, have students share what they learned. Have each presenter add his or her information to a class time line that will show how long it took for his ideas to be realized.

Cross-Curricular Connections

1. ☽☽ *Social studies:* A Renaissance man (or woman) is someone who excels in many fields. Ask students to nominate individuals who are currently living for a modern-day Renaissance person award. Have students present a justification for their nominee. On another day, vote to select one or more winners.

2. ☽☽ *Mathematics:* Have students follow the directions on pp. 34–36 to create a variety of polyhedra (three-dimensional polygons) from small marshmallows and toothpicks. Three examples are shown in the text. Challenge students to come up with others. To extend this activity, ask students to research the work of Luca Pacioli, who shared Leonardo's interest in the connection between art and mathematics. Their findings can be shared orally or in writing.

3. ☽ or ☽☽ *The arts:* Have students research Leonardo's role in the creation of the art form known as "intarsia." Find examples of intarsia in

books or online. Allow interested students to use different shades of paper to simulate the intarsia designs or, if possible, create simple wood mosaics.

Suggested Text Set for Further Discoveries

Casey, Susan. (2005). *Kids Inventing! A Handbook for Young Inventors*. Hoboken, NJ: John Wiley. (NF)

Edwards, Roberta, and True Kelley. (2005). *Who Was Leonardo da Vinci?* Illustrated by True Kelley. New York: Grosset & Dunlap. (B)

Fortey, Jacqueline. (2007). *Great Scientists*. New York: DK Publishing. (NF)

Fritz, Jean, and Hudson Talbott. (2001). *Leonardo's Horse*. Illustrated by Hudson Talbott. New York: Putnam. (NF)

Scieszka, Jon, and Adam McCauley. (2004). *Da Wild, Da Crazy, da Vinci (Time Warp Trio)*. Illustrated by Adam McCauley. New York: Viking. (FYA)

Visconti, Guido, and Bimba Landmann. (2000). *The Genius of Leonardo*. Illustrated by Bimba Landmann. New York: Barefoot Books. (B)

 ### Amazing Journey: Inside the Human Body

Walker, Richard. (2007). *Ouch! How Your Body Makes It through a Very Bad Day*. New York: DK. (NF/PB)

What happens when you sneeze? How does your skin react to sunlight when you get a tan? What defenses does the body use to protect against disease? These and many other questions are answered by Walker's fascinating book. The illustrations steal the show with a range of full-color, computer-generated images that will astound students (and occasionally generate the "yuck" reaction). Those fantastic photos are accompanied by captions, labels, and short text boxes to explain just what's going on inside the human body. And if students want to know more, an enclosed CD presents awesome animations of the events described in the book. A table of contents, glossary, and index help make this a great reference book.

Activity Suggestions

1. ☻ *Take a closer look:* For a fun look inside the human body, show clips from the 1966 film *Fantastic Voyage* (Twentieth Century Fox). Compare movie footage to views from Walker's text. How accurate was the movie? Note: A remake is due in 2010. You could also compare the two versions.

2. ☻☻ *The right tools:* Borrow some health-care tools: stethoscope, blood pressure cuff, and the like. Teach students how to use them. Let them learn to listen to their hearts and take their own pulse and blood pressure. Have

students research the origin of these tools to find out who invented them and when, as well as what methods were used prior to their invention. Assign several students to research each tool. The next day, those with the same assigned tool can meet to prepare short presentations for the class.

3. ☺☺ *Down with bacteria:* Methicillin-resistant Staphylococcus aureus (MRSA) is a timely topic for students to discuss. Have them use the Internet to find out the truth about this bacterium that has been in the news. Discuss preventive measures anyone can take. Assign students to develop brochures informing others about how to deal with MRSA.

4. ☺☺ *You are what you eat:* With obesity on the rise among children, it's appropriate for students to consider what they eat. Have them keep a food log (type of food and amount) for a specific number of days. They can then figure the number of calories consumed per day and the average over the specified period. They can compare that to the number of calories required to maintain a satisfactory weight. For a math connection, have students figure the percentage of healthy versus nonhealthy calories they consume.

Cross-Curricular Connections

1. ☺ *Language arts:* After students have studied the book, use the CD that comes with it. Show one or more animations (no sound). Ask students to write down what is happening in the animation. Students in pairs or small groups can compare what they wrote and judge the accuracy of their writing.

2. ☺ or ☺☺ *Mathematics:* The human body offers opportunities for numerous math applications. For example, the author says an individual's heart beats an average of 100,800 times a day. Based on this number, ask students to estimate how many times their hearts have beaten so far in their lives. Students can solve this problem, too: If a normal heartbeat is about seventy beats per minute, and an adrenalin rush can increase that to 180, what is the percent of increase? Here's a third topic: The author says 4,000 gallons of blood pass through the body each day, maintaining this is enough to fill one hundred bathtubs. Ask students how they could check the accuracy of that statement. Extend this activity by having students create problems to present and solve in class on another day.

3. ☺☺ *The arts:* Students often make decisions that impact their health, now and in the future. Brainstorm a list of these decisions (e.g., smoking, taking drugs or alcohol, body piercing, tattoos, etc.). Ask small groups to

research the health risks of their assigned topics and then create comic strips that could help their fellow students make informed health decisions.

Suggested Text Set for Further Discoveries

Davies, Nicola, and Neal Layton. (2007). *What's Eating You? Parasites—The Inside Story*. Illustrated by Neal Layton. Cambridge, MA: Candlewick Press. (NF)

Giblin, James Cross, and Erik Brooks. (2008). *Did Fleming Rescue Churchill? A Research Puzzle*. Illustrated by Erik Brooks. New York: Henry Holt. (FYA)

Giblin, James Cross, and Michael Dooling. (2006). *The Boy Who Saved Cleveland: Based on a True Story*. Illustrated by Michael Dooling. New York: Henry Holt. (NF)

Jeffrey, Gary. (2007). *Medical Breakthroughs*. Graphic Discoveries. Illustrated by Terry Riley. New York: Rosen Central. (NF)

McClafferty, Carla Killough. (2001). *The Head Bone's Connected to the Neck Bone: The Weird, Wacky, and Wonderful X-Ray*. New York: Farrar, Straus, and Giroux. (NF)

Parsons, Jayne. (2002). *Encyclopedia of the Human Body*. New York: DK Publishing. (NF)

 ## Technology Design: Cool Stuff!

Woodford, Chris, and Jon Woodcock. (2007). *Cool Stuff 2.0 and How It Works*. New York: DK Publishing. (NF/PB)

Ever wonder how a barcode scanner works? How about the recently retired Stealth bomber? What technology goes into making sneakers? These and many more explanations are provided in this colorful and intriguing book. Multiple topics within various chapters are sure to find interest for an entire classroom of students. Topics include how we live (such as hydroponics or bioplastics), connect (Wi-Fi and petcams), play, move, explore, construct, and protect our world. Loaded with graphics, photos, drawings, diagrams, and many more visuals, this book brings common technology to an understandable level in visually exciting ways. A useful glossary is included.

Activity suggestions

1. 🙂🙂 *Hand me that screwdriver:* Many of the illustrations in the book show the internal workings of common electronics. Find defunct (or no

longer in use) electronics that students can dismantle and examine. Create drawings of the inner workings.

2. ☺☺ *BOING:* The Flybar pogo stick is shown on pages 82 and 83. The text explains that changing the length of the piston can change the height of the bounce. First, have students investigate the workings of a piston. Using a prediction/outcome graphic organizer (See Appendix B), have them make predictions related to changes in the piston.

3. ☺☺ *Magnetic attraction:* What do a rail system in China and a floating bed have in common? Magnets! Using pages 16 and 17, have students explore the concepts of magnetic fields. Have them design their own "floating" objects.

4. ☺☺ *I have plenty of energy:* Throughout the book, energy in different forms is discussed in relation to specific technologies. Have students draw proposed designs of technologies we need using alternative energies. For instance, can they develop a solar-powered CD player? Can they use wind power to make their bicycle pedal-free?

Cross-Curricular Connections

1. ☺☺ *Language arts:* The book ends with "What's next"—a perfect organizer for students to write their own science fiction stories. Robots, flying cars, exoskeletons, and many more provide wonderful frameworks for fantasies about the future.

2. ☺ *Mathematics:* Ask students to propose future technology advancements. Vote on the top six and have students interview a specific number of people to get their opinions. Combine the data and create and interpret graphs. Find the mean, median, and mode for the data.

3. ☺☺ *The arts:* In the chapter called "Construct," various structures are examined. Have the students do further research on the buildings presented in "Grand Designs." What objects of nature were used to inspire these? Are there more buildings they can find similar to these?

Suggested Text Set for Further Discoveries

St. George, Judith, and David Small. (2002), *So You Want to Be an Inventor?* Illustrated by David Small. New York: Philomel Books. (NF)

Stiekel, Bettina. (2003). *The Nobel Book of Answers: The Dalai Lama, Mikhail Gorbachev, Shimon Peres, and Other Nobel Prize Winners Answer Some of Life's Most Intriguing Questions for Young People.* New York: Atheneum Books for Young Readers. (B)

Swerling, Lisa, Ralph Lazar, and Jilly McLeod. (2006). *How Nearly Everything Was Invented . . . by the Brainwaves*. New York: DK Publishing. (NF)

Thimmesh, Catherine, and Melissa Sweet. (2000). *Girls Think of Everything: Stories of Ingenious Inventions by Women*. Illustrated by Melissa Sweet. Boston: Houghton Mifflin. (NF)

Woodford Chris. (2008). *Cool Stuff Exploded: Get Inside Modern Technology*. New York: DK Publishing. (NF)

Wyckoff, Edwin Brit. (2008). *The Teen Who Invented Television: Philo T. Farnsworth and His Awesome Invention*. Berkeley Heights, NJ: Enslow. (B)

 ## Rocks and Minerals: Salt

Kurlansky, Mark, and S. D. Schindler. (2006). *The Story of Salt*. Illustrated by S. D. Schindler. New York: G. P. Putnam's Sons. (NF/PB)

Salt is something we use so routinely that it may seem like a very uninteresting topic. And yet, according to the author, it is the only rock humans need to eat in order to live; it made exploration of the earth possible because foods could be cured with salt; and it was a staple of trade for ancient civilizations. Salt has even been "the object of wars and revolutions" (p. 5). Kurlansky hooks the reader with a story about a mysterious pink rock he brought home from Spain and then keeps us interested in learning more about the compound produced from "a metal so unstable that it easily bursts into flame, [combined] with chlorine, a deadly poisonous gas" (p. 6). (Did I mention we have to *eat* salt to live?) Among the helpful features in this book are informative sidebars, maps, and a time line that starts way back in 9750 BCE. Illustrator S. D. Schindler's detailed color pictures add interest and humor as they enhance the reader's understanding of the text.

Activity Suggestions

1. ☺ *Please pass the salt:* Have students examine canned foods to see whether they include salt. (Most do.) Provide an opportunity for students to taste two versions of the same brand of canned vegetables—one with salt, one without. How many of them prefer the unsalted variety? Make a comparison chart showing the number of grams of salt in a serving of various canned foods.

2. ☺☺ *Can I get a fill up?* The author suggests that oil and gas may be found next to a "salt dome." Research the locations of salt domes and oil/gas deposits. (Small groups can be assigned specific areas.) Then, locate them on a map. Ask students what patterns they can see. Discuss whether or not the author is correct.

3. ☻☻ *Home grown:* Salt crystals can easily be grown by stirring salt into boiling water until the liquid reaches the saturation point (see Appendix B). Experiment with different kinds of salt and water to see what happens or try making sugar crystals to generate comparisons. Have students use magnifying glasses to observe the crystalline shapes.

4. ☻☻ *Inquiring minds want to know:* Humans eat salt every day. However, students may be surprised to learn that salt is used for many other things as well. This includes (among others) producing chemicals, deicing of icy surfaces, softening of hard water, seeding of clouds to generate rain, and manufacturing of paper. Have students research the other uses of salt and write a short paper on the one they find to be most useful, most surprising, etc.

Cross-Curricular Connections

1. ☻ *Language arts:* Have students investigate the meaning of the English idiom "salt of the earth" when referring to certain individuals. Discuss what it means and why people with these positive personal qualities would be compared to salt. Then, ask each student to write about someone who possesses those qualities. They could either choose a real person or create a fictional character. If desired, students may share their writing orally.

2. ☻☻ *Mathematics:* The recommended daily allowance for sodium is 2,400 milligrams. Have students solve this problem: If table salt is 40 percent sodium, what quantity of table salt can an individual safely consume in a given day? Collect labels from a variety of processed foods. Fold them so the salt content is not visible. Have small groups of students use the labels to create menus for sample meals. Then, ask each group to calculate the total amount of salt in their meals. Have each group write math problems related to their sample meals. Students can exchange problems and solve them, either individually or as a group.

3. ☻☻ *The arts:* Help students make sculptures from salt dough by mixing flour, salt, and water (see Appendix B). Items also may be painted with tempera paints.

Suggested Text Set for Further Discoveries

Bailey, Jacqui, and Matthew Lilly. (2006). *The Rock Factory: The Story about the Rock Cycle.* Illustrated by Matthew Lilly. Minneapolis, MN: Picture Window Books. (NF)

Cooper, John A. (2002). *Planet Earth & Art Activities.* Arty Facts. Illustrated by Jan Smith. New York: Crabtree. (NF)

Faulkner, Rebecca. (2007). *Crystals.* Geology Rocks! Chicago, IL: Raintree. (NF)

French, Vivian, and Patrice Aggs. (1993). *Why the Sea Is Salt.* Illustrated by Patrice Aggs. Cambridge, MA: Candlewick Press. (FT)

Pellant, Chris. (2002). *Rocks & Minerals.* Smithsonian Handbooks. New York: Dorling Kindersley. (NF)

Zronik, John Paul. (2004). *Salt.* Rocks, Minerals, and Resources. New York: Crabtree. (NF/PB)

 ### Forming the Land: What Lies Beneath

Donovan-O'Meara, Donna, and Stephen James O'Meara. (2005). *Into the Volcano: A Volcano Researcher at Work.* Photographs by Stephen and Donna O'Meara. Toronto, ON: Kids Can Press. (NF/PB)

Donna Donovan-O'Meara has chosen one of the most exciting and dangerous careers possible. She is a volcano researcher. Often, her work takes her to the very lip of an active volcano. The result is a series of color photographs that are both informative and awe-inspiring. Though the narrative descriptions of her life and work are most compelling, the many information boxes sprinkled throughout the book also add interest. These are filled with diagrams, text, and additional photos that explain how volcanoes form, the various types of lava, and the like. A table of contents, glossary, and index increase the book's accessibility. Even the most reluctant learner will be tempted by this real-life adventure.

Activity Suggestions

1. ☻ *Thick, rich, gooey:* The force of eruption is related to the viscosity of the lava. Have students compare how various liquids move down an inclined plane. Which moves farther and faster—prepared cake batter, molasses, applesauce, or honey? (Let students suggest other possibilities to try.) How will the viscosity of the lava impact the shape of the volcano itself?

2. ☻ *In the news:* Earthquakes have shaken the earth numerous times in recent years. Have students map the earth's plate boundaries and then add the locations of recent quakes. Discuss how earthquakes and volcanoes are related to one another.

3. ☻ *Vicarious experience:* The National Geographic photo gallery offers a collection of amazing color pictures showing a variety of adventurous activities and events, including volcanic eruptions and volcano explorations. Access this site at http://photography.nationalgeographic.com/photography/photogalleries to give students additional experiences with volcanoes.

4. ☻ or ☻☻ *Comparisons:* The Volcanic Explosivity Index (VEI) rates the power of an eruption. Values range from zero to eight. Have students check the VEI of recent volcanic eruptions. Find out which were the most powerful and the least powerful. Graph the loss of life and economic losses associated with each incident. To extend this activity, have students compare the human and economic losses of volcanic eruptions with those resulting from other natural disasters, such as hurricanes, tsunamis, tornadoes, etc. Discuss the indices that rate the destructive power of these events.

Cross-Curricular Connections

1. ☻ *Language arts:* Read poems from *Earthshake: Poems from the Ground Up* (see following text set). Then, give students a list of terminology related to volcanoes (e.g., *caldera, dormant, tectonic plate*) and have them write their own poems about volcanoes and their eruptions.

2. ☻ *Social studies:* Landforms can influence population distribution and settlement patterns. Using a world map, have students mark the ten most active volcanoes. Then, have them represent the population living near each of those areas (e.g., using one red dot for every X people). Discuss why people would live near an active volcano. Discuss the other factors that compensate for the danger and how those factors are related to economics.

3. ☻☻ *The arts:* Active volcanoes call to mind hot colors, while dormant ones remind us of cooler hues. Have students use the color palette of their choice to create a painting of these unpredictable landforms.

Suggested Text Set for Further Discoveries

Farndon, John. (2003). *Volcanoes & Earthquakes and Other Facts about Planet Earth.* Bulletpoints. Great Bardfield, UK: Miles Kelly. (NF)

Grace, Catherine O'Neill. (2004). *Forces of Nature: The Awesome Power of Volcanoes, Earthquakes, and Tornadoes.* Washington, DC: National Geographic. (NF)

Levy, Janey. (2008). *World's Worst Volcanic Eruptions.* New York: PowerKids Press. (NF)

Peters, Andrew Fusek. (2007). *Poems about Fire.* London: Evans Brothers. (P)

Peters, Lisa Westberg, and Cathie Felstead. (2003). *Earthshake: Poems from the Ground Up.* Illustrated by Cathie Felstead. New York: Greenwillow Books. (P)

Waldron, Melanie. (2007). *Volcanoes.* Mapping Earthforms. Illustrated by Jeff Edwards. Chicago: Heinemann Library. (NF)

Additional Cross-Curricular Connections

Find more science activities under these featured language arts books (Chapter 2):

> *Lucy Maud Montgomery: The Author of* Anne of Green Gables (Wallner, 2006)
>
> *How to Write Stories: Pin Your Ideas to the Page!* (Warren, 2007)
>
> *A Crossing of Zebras: Animal Packs in Poetry* (Maddox, 2008)
>
> *My Librarian Is a Camel: How Books Are Brought to Children around the World* (Ruurs, 2005)
>
> *The Titanic: An Interactive History Adventure* (Temple, 2008)

Find more science activities under these featured social studies books (Chapter 3):

> *Warriors: All the Truth, Tactics, and Triumphs of History's Greatest Fighters* (Harpur, 2007)
>
> *Yatandou* (Whelan, 2007)
>
> *Seven Miles to Freedom: The Robert Smalls Story* (Halfmann, 2008)
>
> *One Well: The Story of Water on Earth* (Strauss, 2007)

Find more science activities under these featured mathematics books (Chapter 4):

> *Twenty-One Elephants and Still Standing* (Prince, 2005)
>
> *Wild Fibonacci: Nature's Secret Code Revealed* (Hulme, 2005)
>
> *Skyscraper* (Curlee, 2007)
>
> *Great Estimations* (Goldstone, 2006)
>
> *The Great Number Rumble: A Story of Math in Surprising Places* (Lee & O'Reilly, 2007)
>
> *The World Record Paper Airplane Book* (Blackburn & Lammers, 2006)
>
> *A Very Improbable Story* (Einhorn, 2008)

Find more science activities under these featured arts books (Chapter 6):

> *Steel Drumming at the Apollo: The Road to Super Top Dog* (Marx, 2007)
>
> *Good Masters! Sweet Ladies! Voices from a Medieval Village* (Schlitz, 2007)
>
> *The Illustrated Book of Ballet Stories* (Newman, 2005)
>
> *Signing for Kids* (Flodin, 2007)

A. *Kamishibai Man* by Allen Say. **B.** *The Pot That Juan Built* by Nancy Andrews-Goebel; illustrated by David Diaz. **C.** *Paper, Scissors, Sculpt! Creating Cut-and-Fold Animals* by Ben A. Gonzales.

6 Extending Creativity with Picture Books in the Arts

Fine art is that in which the hand, the head, and the heart go together.
—John Ruskin

What would we do without the arts? They lift our minds and hearts and souls to another plane. Be it painting, music, dance, or sculpture, the arts in their many forms tap into our affective side in a way no other subject area can. The arts are disciplines in themselves, but they also are another way of exploring academic content. Thus, students can study dance for its own sake or use dance as a medium for expressing knowledge of social studies. Painting can be studied as a means to help students perfect their artistic skills, or it can be a window for understanding mathematics.

One important reason to include the arts is that they support experiences with cultural diversity. Culture comes alive in the drawings and the dramas, the sculptures and the pottery of our ancestors. We find our past in the musical compositions of Bach or Sousa or the Beatles, and we see the impact of those same composers on contemporary works. For students whose culture is rooted in countries other than the United States, the arts can offer a comforting connection to a home culture and a welcoming link to life in a new land. Our heritage is understood, enhanced, and shared through the arts.

And where do picture books fit in? Everywhere! Picture books can provide information about the arts or the individuals who have achieved success in artistic venues. For example, students can explore the "back story" of theater work in *How Does the Show Go on: An Introduction to the Theater* (Schumaker & Kurtti, 2007). Picture books also offer a new look at a familiar topic, so students who already have studied sculpture may be interested in the intricate paper sculptures found in *Paper, Scissors, Sculpt! Creating Cut-and-Fold Animals* (Gonzales, 2005).

The pictures themselves can serve as models of artwork, as in David Diaz's beautiful southwestern art for *The Pot That Juan Built* (Andrews-Goebel, 2002). Similarly, the text can provide material for practice. After reading excerpts from *The Illustrated Book of Ballet Stories* (Newman, 2005), students may write summaries of other ballets or develop dance steps for familiar fairy tales.

Most of all, picture books can be a source of inspiration—to discover one's self, to find connection to others, to create, to keep trying, and to follow our dreams. Our goal in this chapter was to present books that would offer a new look at the arts in many different formats. You'll find books on the theater, storytelling, painting, sculpture, pottery, music, and more. Teachers of content area studies will find numerous ways to bring the arts into their classrooms as well. (See Appendix A for a link to national arts standards).

To extend learning, teachers also can use text sets of related books. For example, Mrs. Olivier integrated the arts into her language arts classroom by including drama. *Good Masters! Sweet Ladies! Voices from a Medieval Village* (Schlitz, 2007) provided opportunities for reading dialogues and also inspired multiple writing topics. As part of the pre-writing process, students deepened their knowledge of the time period by exploring a rich text set of related fiction, nonfiction, poetry, and folk literature.

We "find ourselves" in the practice and the appreciation of the arts. Use the books in this chapter to help your students do just that.

Back Story: Learning about the Theater

Schumacher, Thomas, and Jeff Kurtti. (2007). *How Does the Show Go on? An Introduction to the Theater*. New York: Disney Editions. (NF/PB)

Thomas Schumacher, producer of the Tony Award-winning Broadway musical *The Lion King*, teams up with author Jeff Kurtti to create a fascinating book on dramatic productions. Authentic items from the theater supplement lavish photographs, diagrams, foldouts, and overlays. On page 23, students will find a real (out-of-date) theater ticket. A playbill is inserted between pages 28 and 29, and sample costume sketches are included at page 58. These are just a few examples. The authors explore everything from theater layouts to special effects in this comprehensive book, ending with "theater-speak" (vocabulary) and instructions for putting on a play. Whether a student wants to try his hand at theater work or just loves attending a performance, he or she will find this this book outstanding.

Activity Suggestions

1. ☻ *Who's who in the theater?* Before exploring this book, have students brainstorm a list of theater-related careers. Create a class list. Then, as you go through the book, add the jobs they didn't mention. See how many different theater careers there are.

2. ☺ *I can do that:* Take theater careers a step farther by having students compare and contrast them with more familiar jobs in other fields. Doing Venn diagrams (See Appendix B) can help students see similarities and differences between the work of a carpenter and a prop manager, an electrical engineer and a lighting designer, etc. They may realize they are already developing some of the skills they will need to perform a job in the theater.

3. ☺☺ *Lights! Camera (optional)! Action:* The Lion King originated as an animated film before being produced as a play. Challenge small groups of students to take their favorite cartoon and turn it into an on-stage production. (Students should select just one scene to dramatize.) They can find plenty of detail in this book about what's involved. If possible, videotape the results to let students see how well they've done.

4. ☺☺ *The play's the thing:* Ideally, students would want to take a field trip to a theater to view a production. If possible, arrange for a backstage tour so students also can see what happens behind the scenes. Follow up with an in-class discussion comparing what they saw with what was included in the book.

Cross-Curricular Connections

1. ☺ *Language arts:* Tap into the magical feeling drama engenders in so many theatergoers by having students describe in writing (poetry or prose) their reaction to the book's photographs—or, even better, to an actual production. Challenge students to use language that expresses an emotional response.

2. ☺ or ☺☺ *Social studies:* Have students investigate the history of theater to find out just how innovative *The Lion King* really was. Make a list of theater "firsts." To extend this activity, have students discuss these innovations and their impact on society.

3. ☺ or ☺☺ *Mathematics:* Page 16 of the book gives a great suggestion for designing a theater by using playing cards and jellybeans. Ratchet up the difficulty level by having students calculate how big their theater must be. If a balcony is included, how many seats can be added? What is the percentage increase in the number of seats? Extend this activity by having students project the amount of additional revenue generated by the larger theater over a specific period of time. What factors may "eat up" some of that revenue (e.g., more programs needed, more workers to care for the larger building, etc.)?

Suggested Text Set for Extending Creativity

Aliki. (1999). *William Shakespeare & the Globe*. New York: HarperCollins. (NF)

Blackwood, Gary. (2003). *Shakespeare's Spy*. New York: Dutton Children's Books. (FYA)

Chanda, Justin (Ed). (2008). *Acting Out: Six One-Act Plays! Six Newbery Stars!* New York: Atheneum Books for Young Readers. (AN/plays by six Newbery authors)

Edwards, Julie, Emma Walton Hamilton, and Tony Walton. (2006). *The Great American Mousical*. The Julie Andrews Collection. Illustrated by Tony Walton. New York: HarperCollins. (FPB)

Foster, Cass, and William Shakespeare. (2000). *Sixty-Minute Shakespeare: Hamlet*. Chandler, AZ: Five Star Publications. (FYA/script)

Katz, Leon. (2004). *The Greek Myths: Puppet Plays for Children from Ovid's Metamorphoses*. New York: Applause Theatre and Cinema Books. (AN)

Miller, Kimberly M. (2003). *Backstage at a Play*. High Interest Books. New York: Children's Press. (NF)

The Art of Japanese Storytelling

Say, Allen. (2005). *Kamishibai Man*. Boston: Houghton Mifflin. (FPB)

Caldecott Award winner Allen Say has created a wonderful book about a very special kind of storytelling. In Japan, "kamishibai" (or "paper theater") was a popular form of entertainment during the early twentieth century. Candy vendors, traveling by bicycle, would signal their arrival by clacking two wooden blocks together. Children would gather to buy candy, much as they do today when they hear the ice cream truck. And the vendor would reward his customers by telling them a story. His tools were a special stage mounted on his bicycle and a set of story cards (sequential pictures, each with text on the back for the "storyteller" to read). *Kamishibai Man* is pulled from Say's childhood memories of Japan and is accompanied by his trademark pastel pictures. Use this book to share a piece of history.

Activity Suggestions

1. ☯ *What's the difference?* To help students better understand the uniqueness of kamishibai, have small groups create charts that compare and contrast this art form with conventional theater or storytelling. Before students begin, have the whole group choose categories for comparison (e.g., number of participants, how the audience is selected, etc.).

2. ☺ *What gets YOUR attention?* Lead a whole-group discussion on entertainment activity choices. What kinds of stories (movies, television, etc.) still get their attention? What, if anything, has replaced TV in their lives? Discuss what factors influence them to choose one form of activity over another. Can they see any implications for the future of performance entertainment?

3. ☺☺ *Story, please:* Have students create a set of story cards for a favorite tale. Each would have a picture on the front and text on the back. Be sure they number them correctly. (The text for card 1 is actually on the back of the final picture, and so on—See Appendix B.) The next day, let students use the cards to present their stories to the class.

4. ☺☺ *On the road:* Turn students into traveling storytellers by allowing them to perform their own kamishibai stories in other classrooms. Students in early elementary grades will be charmed by the entertainment.

Cross-Curricular Connections

1. ☺☺ *Language arts:* Awaken an interest in storytelling by asking students to chronicle some of the stories that have been passed down in their own families. Each student could summarize the story and write what they know about its origin and its importance to their family. To integrate technology, create an online "book" that students can share. Parents could access it from home as well.

2. ☺☺ *Social studies:* Kamishibai disappeared because of the advent of television. Have students interview parents (or even grandparents) about changes in employment during their lives. Were any of these changes due to technological advances? Students' reports can be made orally or in writing.

3. ☺ or ☺☺ *Mathematics*: Have the students bring in favorite candy recipes. For each recipe, calculate the amount of each ingredient needed to create enough candy to accommodate a given number of customers. To extend this activity, have students check prices and then calculate the price to make candy for the same number of customers. Compare. Decide which candy recipe is most cost-effective.

Suggested Text Set for Extending Creativity

Behnke, Alison. (2002). *Japan in Pictures*. Visual Geography Series. Minneapolis, MN: Lerner Publications. (NF)

Blake, Dorothy. (2005). *A Shower of All My Days: Selected Haikus and Others Taken from "Haiku Apprenticeship—2003–2004."* Lincoln, NE: iUniverse. (P)

Forest, Heather, and David Boston. (1995). *Wonder Tales from around the World.* Little Rock, AR: August House. (AN/FT)

Sakade, Florence. (2008). *Kintaro's Adventures and Other Japanese Children's Favorite Stories.* Illustrated by Yoshio Hayashi. Tokyo, Japan: Tuttle Publishing. (AN/FT)

Spivak, Dawnine, and Demi. (1997). *Grass Sandals: The Travels of Basho.* Illustrated by Demi. New York: Atheneum Books for Young Readers. (B)

Yolen, Jane, and Raúl Colón. (2003). *Mightier Than the Sword: World Folktales for Strong Boys.* Illustrated by Raúl Colón. San Diego, CA: Harcourt. (FT)

Musical Dreams: The Audition

Marx, Trish, and Ellen B. Senisi. (2007). *Steel Drumming at the Apollo: The Road to Super Top Dog.* Photographs by Ellen Senisi. New York: Lee & Low Books. (NF/PB)

Author Trish Marx profiles seven talented musicians from Schenectady, New York. They are high school friends who came together to form the Hamilton Hill Steel Drum Band. Their goal: to qualify for the Top Dog competition at the world famous Apollo Theater in New York City. Marx chronicles the group's journey through winning a local competition, making the next level cut, and ultimately competing in the Amateur Night Show-Off at the Apollo. To provide more information, the author includes sidebars about steel drums, the Apollo Theater, and more. Color photos by Ellen Senisi, mother of one of the band members, capture the excitement of the Apollo experience and bring the story to life. And to bring the music to life, the publisher has included a CD featuring their steel drum audition piece, plus music by each of the seven young performers. This is a book to inspire dreams of success!

Activity Suggestions

1. ☻ *Hands on:* Bring in a range of percussion instruments for students to try. If possible, include a steel drum and compare its mellow tone to that made by other kinds of percussion instruments. Ask students which sounds they like best and why. Do they see specific uses for certain percussion instruments (e.g., does one instrument set a different mood than another one does)?

2. ☻☻ *Time for music:* Take students to an orchestral performance to challenge their ideas about the life of a musician. Arrange for one or more of the performers to talk with students afterwards about their own journey to becoming a successful musician. Have students prepare questions

ahead of time. After the interview, ask students to write about something they learned.

3. ☻☻ *Dream a little dream:* Have students follow the progress of their favorite contestant or contestants on a reality talent show (e.g., *American Idol, America's Got Talent*, etc.). Have them compare the steps these artists are following with those taken by the musicians in the book.

4. ☻☻ *Amateur night:* Stage your own "musical amateur night" with student volunteers performing as musicians or providing accompaniment for those who prefer to sing or dance. Students who do not want to perform can offer off-stage assistance.

Cross-Curricular Connections

1. ☻ *Language arts:* Read the poem *The Dream Keeper* by Langston Hughes. What does he mean by "heart melodies"? This metaphor is uniquely suited for the dreams of the members of Hamilton Hill Steel Drum Band. Have students create metaphors to describe the dreams of singers, dancers, or other performers—or their own dreams.

2. ☻ or ☻☻ *Social studies:* Steel drums are evocative of the Caribbean. Locate Trinidad and Tobago on a globe. Find out what other countries are also considered part of the Caribbean. Listen to music by artists from this part of the world and decide what characteristics make this music unique. To extend this activity, ask students to bring in examples of contemporary popular music that have a Caribbean flavor.

3. ☻☻ *Science:* Investigate the making of steel drum instruments. Find out whether or how technology has changed the way these drums are made. Although panmakers take up to ten years to learn the technique of making a steel drum, students can experiment with shaping metal by creating a "dudup." This early instrument can be made with an inverted coffee can or paint can. Draw a line across the bottom (not quite down the middle—make the two resulting surfaces different in size.) Pound on the line with a hammer (can be a new pencil with a hard eraser or a dowel rod wrapped with rubber bands). The two surfaces should make different notes. Ask students to predict which note will be higher (the smaller surface). Various websites tell more about making a dudup. One of them is http://gamma.sitelutions.com/~toucans/Toc/makeYourOwn.html. Students who are interested in metallurgy as a possible career can research more about the shaping of metal.

Suggested Text Set for Extending Creativity

Hernandez, Romel. (2009). *Trinidad and Tobago*. Philadelphia: Mason Crest. (NF)

Hughes, Langston, and J. Brian Pinkney. (2007). *The Dream Keeper and Other Poems*. Illustrated by J. Brian Pinkney. New York: Knopf. (P)

Nathan, Amy. (2006). *Meet the Musicians: From Prodigy (or Not) to Pro*. New York: Henry Holt. (NF)

Nathan, Amy. (2008). *Meet the Dancers: From Ballet, Broadway, and Beyond*. New York: Henry Holt. (NF)

Ryan, Pam Muñoz, and Brian Selznick. (2002). *When Marian Sang: The True Recital of Marian Anderson: The Voice of a Century*. Illustrated by Brian Selznick. New York: Scholastic Press. (B)

Scott, Justin. (2008). *The Drummer's Bible*. Secaucus, NJ: Chartwell Books. (NF)

Scrapbook Memoirs: History through the Visual Arts

Williams, Marcia. (2007). *Archie's War: My Scrapbook of the First World War, 1914-1918*. Cambridge, MA: Candlewick Press. (FPB)

Archie Albright is ten-years-old when he starts his comic book scrapbook in 1914. Living in London, England, Archie is a typical boy of the times. We meet his family and see his school, his "mates," and the first signs that war is pending. By August, England is engaged in a war with Germany, but many claim it will be over by Christmas. An armistice is signed four years later. Through Archie's comic book scrapbook (which includes fold-out sections, letters in envelopes, postcards, and many more dimensional works), we see the unfolding of the war, the loss of his uncle, the bombing of his friend's home, and his father's eventual return from the war. Packed with visuals, this book not only expands students' knowledge about the use of media but also about World War I.

Activity Suggestions

1. ☻☻ *Into the third dimension:* Archie uses a number of media to create his cartoon scrapbook. How did the author achieve the "dimensional" look on some of the pages? Discuss the use of photographing collage pages to create illustrations for a book (Jeannie Baker used this medium frequently in such books as *Window* [1991] and *Where the Forest Meets the Sea* [1987]). Have students analyze and reproduce these with their own drawings.

2. ☻☻ *Story frames:* Use one of the comic panels to examine how Archie develops a short story on a page. Have students draw characters and provide dialogue to tell a story, comic-strip style.

3. ☺☺ *Tin memoirs:* Archie creates a rubbing of his dad's tobacco tin (which hides notes from his dad when he was on the front). Have students decide how Archie created the rubbing and invite them to bring "treasures" from home to replicate Archie's tin rubbing.

4. ☺☺ *Papermaking:* Many of the pages differ in color and appearance. During war times, items like paper, crayons, and pencils became difficult to find. Have students make their own paper (see Appendix B) and then use it to create a scrapbook page.

Cross-Curricular Connections

1. ☺☺ *Language arts:* British English words are used throughout the book. Have students find the words and use the glossary to examine their meanings. Discuss which words they could figure out from context. Are there other books (such as the Harry Potter series) that use terms the students do not use on a regular basis? The front matter of dictionaries gives information about American English and British English differences. Research Noah Webster and the purposeful changes he made to differentiate American English from British English.

2. ☺☺ *Social studies:* Create a game similar to Jeopardy using the historic facts presented in this fiction text (see http://www.hardin.k12.ky.us/res_techn/countyjeopardygames.htm for a blank PowerPoint program to create the game). You can create it to play with the students or have students work in teams to develop ones to share and play in class.

3. ☺☺ *Mathematics:* Have students investigate the price of specific food items (e.g., sugar, coffee, beef, butter, bread) before and during a war. Small groups could be assigned to research prices during different wars to calculate percentage of increases caused by each war. On another day, compare the increases.

Suggested Text Set for Extending Creativity

Brewster, Hugh. (1996). *Anastasia's Album: The Last Tsar's Youngest Daughter Tells Her Own Story.* New York: Hyperion Books for Children. (NF)

Fleming, Candace. (2005). *Our Eleanor: A Scrapbook Look at Eleanor Roosevelt's Remarkable Life.* New York: Atheneum Books for Young Readers. (NF)

Krull, Kathleen. (2002). *V Is for Victory: America Remembers World War II.* New York: Knopf. (NF)

Price, Pamela S. (2005). *Cool Scrapbooks.* Edina, MN: ABDO Publishing. (NF)

Russo, Marisabina. (2005). *Always Remember Me: How One Family Survived World War II.* New York: Atheneum Books for Young Readers. (B)

Sis, Peter. (2007). *The Wall: Growing Up Behind the Iron Curtain*. New York: Farrar, Straus, and Giroux. (NF/PB)

Williams, Marcia. (2008). *My Secret War Diary, by Flossie Albright: My History of the Second World War, 1939–1945*. Cambridge, MA: Candlewick Press. (NF)

Drama: Exploring Characterization with Monologue and Dialogue

Schlitz, Laura Amy, and Robert Byrd. (2007). *Good Masters! Sweet Ladies! Voices from a Medieval Village*. Illustrated by Robert Byrd. Cambridge, MA: Candlewick Press. (NF/PB)

Lead students to understand the perspectives of multiple characters with this superb collection of monologues. Schlitz has drawn on her love of history and drama to create a series of nineteen plays for single actors (and two dialogues that involve a conversation between two characters). Each brief drama presents the viewpoint of a specific character, one of many fictitious inhabitants of an English manor in the year 1255. The collection in its entirety gives the reader a well-rounded picture of village life in medieval times. Footnotes along the side of each page clarify unfamiliar terms and provide historical context for the reader. At the end of the book, an extensive bibliography documents the author's research. This book is beautifully formatted with lovely color pictures by Robert Byrd.

Activity Suggestions

1. ☺ *Conflicting viewpoints:* Create a wall chart describing the perspectives of the various characters in the book. Do some of the views conflict? If so, how? How does each person's station in life affect his or her views? Challenge students to reflect those perspectives in their oral reading of each selection.

2. ☺ *Characterization times two:* The book includes two dialogues or conversations between two actors. Ask student volunteers to read them aloud. How does the addition of a second voice bring out the personal qualities of each character? Do students prefer the dialogues or the monologues? Why?

3. ☺☺ *Putting them all together:* Select several of the monologues (or dialogues). Write a prologue and connecting passages to create a Readers' Theater (See Appendix B). Have students perform for another class.

4. ☺☺ *Modern times:* Ask students to re-create this book as a modern tale. After generating a list of possible characters, have each student select one

current-day individual (a generic resident of a present-day town—e.g., a doctor, a store keeper, a mail carrier) and write a monologue for him or her. Next step—oral presentations!

Cross-Curricular Connections

1. ☻☻ *Language arts:* Have each student select one monologue and rewrite it as a third-person paragraph. After students share their paragraphs, discuss what was "lost in translation."

2. ☻☻ *Social studies:* Have small groups of students create three-dimensional models of a medieval village. Assign different time periods so students can see how villages progressed over time.

3. ☻ or ☻☻ *Science:* "Drogo, the tanner's apprentice" talks about pollution caused by tanners in medieval times. Ask students to research the making of leather. Are there still pollution issues in this industry? What other industries still have problems with pollution? What has been done to address the problem? To extend this activity, students can make posters to document progress (or the lack of progress) by various industries.

Suggested Text Set for Extending Creativity

Cushman, Karen. (2002). *Matilda Bone*. A Dell Yearling Book. New York: Dell Yearling. (FYA)

Czarnota, Lorna. (2000). *Medieval Tales That Kids Can Read & Tell*. Little Rock, AR: August House. (AN/FT)

Gravett, Christopher. (2008). *Castle*. DK Eyewitness Books. New York: DK Children. (NF)

MacDonald, Fiona, and Adam Hook. (2005). *Town Life*. Medieval World. Illustrated by Adam Hook. North Mankato, MN: Smart Apple Media. (NF)

Steele, Philip, and Steve Noon. (2004). *A City through Time*. Illustrated by Steve Noon. New York: DK Publishing. (NF)

Williams, Marcia, and Geoffrey Chaucer. (2007). *Here Bygynneth Chaucer's Canterbury Tales*. Cambridge, MA: Candlewick Press. (P)

 ## Bravo! Appreciating the Ballet, the Opera, and the Symphony

Newman, Barbara, and Gill Tomblin. (2005). *The Illustrated Book of Ballet Stories*. Illustrated by Gill Tomblin. New York: DK Publishing. (NF/PB)

Students may describe some of the most beautiful music ever written as "old-fashioned" or "boring." Those who are unwilling to give ballet or opera a try may be enticed to listen when they hear the story behind the music. Newman's book provides background information and story lines for five favorite ballets: *The Sleeping Beauty, Giselle, Coppelia, Swan Lake,* and *The Nutcracker*. Stories are divided into four or five short scenes, each with a summary of the events accompanied by color illustrations and color photos of actual performances. Captions explain details of how the dancers tell the story through movement. An introduction illustrates ballet movements, while a glossary explains related terms. This book comes with a CD. Combine it with the text to bring these beautiful stories to life!

Activity Suggestions

1. ☯ *Once upon a time:* Compare the stories in this book to familiar folk tales and fairy tales. Generate a list of commonalities about folk and fairy tales. How many of those same qualities are seen in the stories presented by Newman?

2. ☯☯ *Their turn:* Have small groups of students choose a folk or fairy tale not included in the book. Then, ask them to select music (preferably without words) that expresses the story. Have groups write scripts and perform their stories, accompanied by their music selections.

3. ☯☯ *Just the music:* Some symphonic performances (no dancing, no singing) include music that is also meant to tell a story. *Peter and the Wolf* is a wonderful introduction to symphonic music for young listeners. Take students to a performance. Then, have them suggest instruments that might portray other animals or characters. Students can create short-note sequences to accompany readings of fables or other animal tales.

4. ☯☯ *Adding the words:* Unlike ballet, opera tells the story through both words and melody. *Porgy and Bess* (Samuel Goldwyn, 1959) is performed in English. View the film and then ask students to summarize the story line. How would they rate the importance of the words in portraying the story?

Curricular Connections

1. ☯☯ *Language arts:* Choose a piece of music and have students write stories that express what they hear. On another day, have students read them aloud. Compare the variety of plot lines, characters, and other story aspects generated by students. What elements in the music inspired students' choices?

2. ☯ *Social studies:* Listen to Tchaikovsky's *1812 Overture* as an example of how music was used to interpret real events (Russia's defense against Napoleon in 1812). Discuss what was happening in America at this same

time. Have students write short papers comparing America's War of 1812 with the events that inspired Tchaikovsky.

3. ☺ *Science:* In musical compositions of all kinds, pitch is critical. Explore how sound travels (e.g., by touching a vibrating tuning fork to water). Fill several identical glasses with varying amounts of water. Strike each with the same object and listen to the pitch of the tone. Bring in some musical instruments. Give the students an opportunity to feel the vibrations as each one is played. Compare the size of the instrument with the sound it generates. See if students can draw any generalizations between the size of the instrument and the pitch.

Suggested Text Set for Extending Creativity

Celenza, Anna Harwell, JoAnn E. Kitchel, and Joseph Haydn. (2000). *The Farewell Symphony.* Illustrated by JoAnn E. Kitchel. Watertown, MA: Charlesbridge. (NF)

Ganeri, Anita, and Nicola Barber. (2001). *The Young Person's Guide to the Opera: With Music from the Great Operas on CD.* San Diego: Harcourt. (NF)

Koscielniak, Bruce. (2000). *The Story of the Incredible Orchestra: An Introduction to Musical Instruments and the Symphony Orchestra.* Boston: Houghton Mifflin. (NF)

Shahrukh, Husain, James Mayhew, and Miranda Richardson. (2007). *The Barefoot Book of Stories from the Opera.* Illustrated by James Mayhew. New York: Barefoot Books. (NF)

Siberell, Anne. (2001). *Bravo! Brava! A Night at the Opera: Behind the Scenes with Composers, Cast, and Crew.* Illustrated by Frederica von Stade. New York: Oxford University Press. (NF.)

Yolen, Jane, and Vladimir Vagin. (2002). *The Firebird.* Illustrated by Vladimir Vagin. New York: HarperCollins. (FT)

 ## Pottery: Rediscovering an Ancient Process

Andrews-Goebel, Nancy, and David Diaz. (2002). *The Pot That Juan Built.* Illustrated by David Diaz. Photographs by Nancy Andrews-Goebel and Michael Wisner. New York: Lee & Low Books. (B/PB)

The life of Juan Quezada, the premier potter of Mexico, is explored in this interesting and colorful book. Quezada is credited with discovering the pottery-making process used by an ancient people, the Casas Grandes. Each double-page spread includes information about Quezada's life and potting techniques on the right side, while the left-hand page has a cumulative rhyme: "These are the flames so sizzling hot; That flickered and flared and fired the pot; The beautiful pot that Juan built" (unpaged).

Brilliantly colored illustrations by David Diaz evoke a southwestern feeling. An afterword gives additional information and shows photos of Quezada at work.

Activity Suggestions

1. ☻ or ☻☻ *Another take on pottery:* Online research will help students learn how various ancient peoples made pottery. Have students compare the techniques and critique the results. Discuss which finished products they prefer. Why? As an extension, assign students to research current methods for mass-production of pottery. Have each student choose one method (ancient or modern) and write out the steps. Students who choose the same method should cross-check their directions for correct order and completeness.

2. ☻☻ *Give it a try:* Students will want to make some pottery of their own. If possible, allow them to try out at least two different techniques to get a feel for how they were used. Ask students to comment on whether they find one method more comfortable to use than another.

3. ☻☻ *Adding a Mexican flavor:* Allow students to paint their handmade pottery with authentic Mexican designs. Provide design ideas such as those seen in Cynthia Weill's book in the following list.

4. ☻☻ *A picture is worth a Caldecott Award:* David Diaz won the Caldecott Award for his illustrations in *Smoky Night* (Bunting, 1995). Collect this and other examples of his work, such as *Going Home* (Bunting, 1998) or *Wilma Unlimited: How Wilma Rudolph Became the World's Fastest Woman* (Krull, 2000). Discuss the ethnic feeling of his art. Have students create paintings in that style.

Cross-Curricular Connections

1. ☻☻ *Language arts:* The cumulative rhyme in Andrews-Goebel's book adds interest while it describes the pottery-making process in a new way. Ask students to choose another process (even something as simple as making a sandwich) and write a cumulative rhyme to accompany each step. If desired, students can create their own "how-to" books with informative text on the right and the rhyming text on the facing page.

2. ☻ *Social studies:* Pinpoint the locations of various ancient peoples who were known for their pottery. Ask students to find out what local environmental factors contributed to their ability to create pottery. What kinds of containers were used by other ancient peoples instead of pottery? Again, what environmental factors contributed?

3. ☺ or ☺☺ *Mathematics:* Bring in a variety of pots of conventional shapes (e.g., cylinders of different sizes) and have students develop and use strategies for calculating the volume of each in cubic centimeters. They can convert this number to ounces (1 ounce equals approximately 29.57 cubic centimeters). Afterwards, fill each pot with liquid and measure the actual volume. Compare the result with students' calculations. Discuss the reasons for any discrepancies. For more able students, bring in a pot that combines shapes (e.g., spherical at the bottom and cylindrical at the top) and see if they can develop an equation to calculate the volume. Again, check their accuracy by filling the pot with water and measuring the actual volume.

Suggested Text Set for Extending Creativity

Baylor, Byrd, and Tom Bahti. (1987). *When Clay Sings.* Illustrated by Tom Bahti. New York: Aladdin Books/Macmillan. (FPB)

Chavarría, Joaquim. (1999). *Hand-Building Techniques.* Ceramics Class. New York: Watson-Guptill Publications. (NF)

Ellis, Mary. (2004). *Ceramics for Kids: Creative Clay Projects to Pinch, Roll, Coil, Slam, & Twist.* Asheville, NC: Lark Books. (NF)

Emert, Phyllis Raybin. (2009). *Pottery.* Eye on Art. Detroit, MI: Lucent Books. (NF)

Nierman, Kevin, Elaine Arima, and Curtis H Arima. (2000). *The Kids 'N' Clay Ceramics Book: Handbuilding and Wheel-Throwing Projects from the Kids 'N' Clay Pottery Studio.* Berkeley, CA: Tricycle. (NF)

Weill, Cynthia, K. B. Basseches, Moisés Jiménez, and Armando Jiménez. (2007). *ABeCedarios: Mexican Folk Art ABCs in English and Spanish.* Illustrated by Moisés Jiménez and Armando Jiménez. Photographs by K. B. Basseches. El Paso, TX: Cinco Puntos Press. (ABC)

 ## Moving to Music: American Sign Language

Flodin, Mickey. (2007). *Signing for Kids.* New York: Perigee. (NF/PB)

Music and movement go together, and one of the most beautiful ways to combine them in a meaningful way is with American Sign Language. *Signing for Kids* teaches students to "talk" with their hands, making it possible for them to expressively sign at least some of the words to many songs. Besides the manual alphabet, which is familiar to many people, the book presents eighteen chapters of signing categories (everything from snacks and food to God and religion). An introduction gives general instructions on signing and how to use the book. Clearly drawn diagrams illustrate how to execute each sign, while black-and-white photographs (also by Flodin) add interest to the text.

Activity Suggestions

1. ☉ *Moving examples:* Show students what the finished product might look like by viewing a clip from the movie *Mr. Holland's Opus* (Hollywood Pictures, 1995) in which Richard Dreyfus sings a John Lennon song accompanied by sign language. Another example, a video showing sign language accompanying a group, is *Sister Act II* (Touchstone, 2000). Near the end of the movie, a group of high school students take part in a music competition, very effectively using both sign language and more active movement as they sing.

2. ☉☉ *"Give me an A":* As a starting point for signing to music, teach students the American Sign Language alphabet and let them fingerspell an accompaniment to the old familiar ABC song. Students probably will need to practice at home before attempting to sign the entire alphabet.

3. ☉☉ *It's a matter of choice:* Let each student choose a song he or she would like to accompany with sign language. Have students learn the motions to a portion of the song (e.g., perhaps the chorus) and demonstrate it for the class.

4. ☉☉ *Take action:* After the class has learned to accompany a few songs with sign language, consider a concert for individuals with hearing disabilities. One poignant song choice might be *Don't Laugh at* Me (see text set below). Individuals or the class as a whole can do signing.

Cross-Curricular Connections

1. ☉ *Language arts:* Simulate a hearing disability by showing students a short movie without the sound. Choose a film clip in which the plot is not easily guessed. Make sure the clip includes some conversation and is no more than a few minutes long. Then, have students write down what they think was happening. Students can share orally before they see the film clip a second time with the sound turned on.

2. ☉☉ *Social studies:* Consider the concept of culture in a new light. Introduce students to the concept of the "Deaf Culture" (made up of individuals who are deaf). Define culture and discuss why deafness may be considered a culture in itself. (The book by Kelley, in the following list, may be useful.) Ask each student to write a journal entry from the point of view of someone who is deaf. On another day, discuss which aspects of

life both hearing individuals and individuals with a hearing impairment might experience the same way. What things are different?

3. ☮ *Science:* Let students explore how non-hearing individuals can experience music through vibration. Easy examples may include: touching the throat when singing or humming, touching the surface of a stereo speaker when in use, placing loose paper clips on top of a drum and striking its surface, etc.

Suggested Text Set for Extending Creativity

Alexander, Sally Hobart, and Robert Joseph Alexander. (2008). *She Touched the World: Laura Bridgman, Deaf-Blind Pioneer*. New York: Clarion Books. (B)

Kelley, Walter P., and Tony L. McGregor. (2003). *Deaf Culture A to Z*. Illustrated by Tony Landon McGregor. Austin, TX: Buto, Ltd. (ABC)

Matlin, Marlee. (2004). *Deaf Child Crossing*. New York: Aladdin Paperbacks. (FYA)

McCully, Emily Arnold. (2008). *My Heart Glow: Alice Cogswell, Thomas Gallaudet, and the Birth of American Sign Language*. New York: Hyperion Books for Young Children. (B)

Seskin, Steve, Allen Shamblin, and Glin Dibley. (2002). *Don't Laugh at Me*. Illustrations by Glin Dibley. Berkeley, CA: Tricycle Press. (NF, illustrated song text, CD included)

Uhlberg, Myron, and Henri Sorensen. (2003). *The Printer*. Illustrated by Henri Sorensen. Atlanta, GA: Peachtree. (FPB)

 ## Sculpture: The Shape of Things

Gonzales, Ben A. (2005). *Paper, Scissors, Sculpt! Creating Cut-and-Fold Animals*. New York: Sterling. (NF/PB)

When we think of sculpture, heavy blocks of stone come to mind. However, Ben Gonzales has invented a method of scoring, cutting, and folding paper that will allow students to create beautiful sculptures from paper. "Gupit-Gupit" (pronounced **goo**peet-**goo**peet) requires minimal materials: paper and pencils, scissors, push pins, adhesive, and a mat knife (supervised use only). Helpful illustrations accompany the explanations for using basic techniques. Directions are included for making twenty-two animals, ranging from the very easy snake to the far more complex giraffe. Projects are rated with a star system, from one star for "basic" designs up to four stars for those that are "inspired." The book ends with a photo gallery of complex sculptures, a glossary, and a troubleshooting "paper clinic." What an inexpensive way to learn about sculpture!

Activity Suggestions

1. ☺ or ☺☺ *The next step:* After students have tried some of the designs in this book, challenge students to paper-sculpt an animal that the author has not included. Students should keep a record of the steps they followed (e.g., with photographs accompanied by written instructions). On another day, have students try to reproduce a classmate's design.

2. ☺ or ☺☺ *Keep experimenting:* Have students experiment with the Gupit-Gupit technique. Can they achieve interesting results by using different kinds of paper, by adding color, or by combining paper sculpture with other media? Discuss the aesthetic value of each variation.

3. ☺☺ *It's not set in stone:* While sculpting in stone is not possible for many students, they probably have experience in using papier-mâché, another inexpensive technique using paper. Ask them to create an animal of their choice using this technique. (Ideally, they would choose an animal presented in the book that they already have created using the paper sculpture technique.) Then, evaluate the results. Do students prefer the solidity of the papier-mâché or the detail of the paper sculpture? Are there times when one medium would be preferable to the other? Typically, papier-mâché is built up, while sculpture removes material. Which is easier to control?

4. ☺☺ *Movable sculptures:* In the movie *Twister* (Warner Brothers, 1996), one of the characters creates movable sculptures called mobiles (see text set). Show a brief clip from the movie for inspiration. Then, allow students to choose their own materials and experiment with "kinetic art." Display finished pieces and allow students to discuss and evaluate their aesthetic qualities.

Cross-Curricular Connections

1. ☺☺ *Language arts:* Use this book's emphasis on shapes as an opportunity to introduce (or review) shape poems, in which the shape of the words on the page reinforces the meaning of the poem (see Appendix B). For example, a student writing about a snake could let his words coil around the page. For a three-dimensional shape poem, have students create simple animal sculptures and then write their poems on their animals.

2. ☺☺ *Social studies:* Have students make dioramas (miniature frozen scenes) of historic events. Use of the paper sculpture technique means students are not limited to action figures and dime-store miniatures in their choice of objects to include in their scenes. Discuss their use of materials.

3. ☻ *Mathematics:* The designs in the book offer a perfect opportunity to discuss symmetry. After viewing the author's animal designs, have students examine a variety of geometric shapes to determine whether they are symmetrical. Can students find the lines of symmetry in each one? Have them combine tangram pieces (or geometric shapes cut from paper) to create a shape that is symmetrical and one that is not.

Suggested Text Set for Extending Creativity

Barton, Carol. (2005). *The Pocket Paper Engineer. How to Make Pop-Ups Step-By-Step. Vol. 1: Basic Forms.* Glen Echo, MD: Popular Kinetics Press. (NF)

Barton, Carol. (2008). *The Pocket Paper Engineer. How to Make Pop-Ups Step-By-Step. Vol. 2: Platforms & Props.* Glen Echo, MD: Popular Kinetics Press. (NF)

Garza, Carmen Lomas. (1999). *Making Magic Windows: Creating Cut-Paper Art with Carmen Lomas Garza.* San Francisco, CA: Children's Book Press. (NF)

Maurer-Mathison, Diane V. (2006). *Paper in Three Dimensions: Origami, Pop-Ups, Sculpture, Baskets, Boxes, and More.* New York: Watson-Guptill. (NF)

Nakazawa, Keiko, and Yoko Ishiguro. (2006). *3D Pop-Up Greeting Cards.* Tokyo: Japan Publications Trading. (NF)

Rose, Timothy. (2007). *Making Creative Mobiles.* Bloomington, IN: AuthorHouse. (NF)

Sabuda, Robert, C. S. Lewis, and Matthew S. Armstrong. (2007). The Chronicles of Narnia *Pop-Up.* New York: HarperCollins. (FPB)

Wood, Dorothy. (2007). *Paper Pop Up: 40 Dynamic Designs for Surprising Cards and Gifts.* Cincinnati, OH: David & Charles. (NF)

 ## Exploring Abstract Art

Raimondo, Joyce. (2008). *What's the Big Idea? Activities and Adventures in Abstract Art.* New York: Watson-Guptill Publications. (NF/PB)

This wonderfully colorful book encourages students to explore the techniques used by six well-known abstract artists—Picasso, Matisse, Leger, O'Keeffe, Calder, and Gorky. Raimondo provides a short description of each artist's work, accompanied by an example of his or her art. Questions help the reader analyze the artwork. Then, the fun begins as the author suggests activities that will allow students to try those same techniques in creating their own art. Photographs of artwork done by students (ages eight through twelve) present some of the possibilities that may be achieved. Text boxes give details about artists' work or offer suggestions for comparing the work of various artists. At the end of the book, brief biographies of the six featured artists offer additional information.

Activity Suggestions

1. ☺☺ *Make your own choices:* Like that of Fernand Leger, Piet Mondrian's work makes use of "hard-edge" painting. However, he limits color choices to red, yellow, and blue, together with black, white, and gray. Share some examples of his work. Challenge students to create a Mondrian-like painting with their own choice of colors. Compare the results.

2. ☺☺ *Picasso, please:* Have students create a Picasso-like "masterpiece" by cutting photographs of faces from magazines. They can then glue the pieces together to create a new face seen from multiple viewpoints.

3. ☺☺ *Art elements:* According to the author, "abstract artists explore the elements of art—line, shape, color, pattern, texture, and form—as subjects in their own right" (p. 5). Ask students to choose one of the six elements and find out how it is used by artists not included in the book (need not be abstract art). Students can create comparison charts to show what they learned.

4. ☺☺ *You have the floor:* Artist Jackson Pollock placed large canvases on the floor and created art which he called "energy and motion made visible" (Greenberg & Jordan, 2002, p. 29). Have students research his painting style and then let small groups collaborate on large-scale paintings that are done on the floor. Let them experiment with how the paint could be applied to the canvas through "energy and motion."

Cross-Curricular Connections

1. ☺ or ☺☺ *Language arts:* Display several examples of abstract art. Ask each student to select one and write a paragraph or two about what he or she thinks it represents. Extend the activity by letting students exchange paragraphs and try to guess which example is being interpreted.

2. ☺☺ *Social studies:* Where and when did each of the six featured artists live and work? What was each person's nationality? Have students learn more about the time period or periods in question, choose one artist, and write opinion papers about the social conditions that supported his or her art form.

3. ☺☺ *Mathematics:* Put math in motion by creating Calder-like mobiles of geometric shapes. Use the photo of "Myxamatose" (p. 27) as a model for inspiration. Then, ask students to choose a shape other than a circle to complete their mobiles. Provide a wide variety of materials for students to use. To make it more challenging, have them consider issues such as

repeated patterns (e.g., the diameter of the square increases or decreases at a specific rate) or symmetry.

Suggested Text Set for Extending Creativity

Greenberg, Jan, Sandra Jordan, and Robert Andrew Parker. (2002). *Action Jackson.* Illustrated by Robert Andrew Parker. Brookfield, CT: Roaring Brook Press. (B/PB)

Jacobson, Rick, and Laura Fernandez. (2004). *Picasso: Soul on Fire.* Illustrated by Laura Fernandez. Toronto, ON: Tundra Books. (B/PB)

Johnson, Stephen T. (2008). *A Is for Art: An Abstract Alphabet.* Illustrated by Stephen T. Johnson. New York: Simon & Schuster Books for Young Readers. (ABC)

Kelley, True, and Pablo Picasso. (2002). *Pablo Picasso: Breaking All the Rules, by Simon Packard.* Smart about Art. New York: Penguin. (B/PB)

O'Connor, Jane, and Jessie Hartland. (2002). *Henri Matisse: Drawing with Scissors.* Smart about Art. Illustrated by Jessie Hartland. New York: Penguin. (B/BP)

Wolfe, Gillian. (2002). *Look! Zoom in on Art!* Oxford, England: Oxford University Press. (NF/PB)

Additional Cross-Curricular Connections

Find more arts activities under these featured language arts books (Chapter 2):

Louis Sockalexis: Native American Baseball Pioneer (Wise, 2007)

How to Write Stories: Pin Your Ideas to the Page! (Warren, 2007)

The Girl's Like Spaghetti: Why, You Can't Manage without Apostrophes! (Truss, 2007)

You Let the Cat Out of the Bag! (And Other Crazy Animal Sayings) (Klingel, 2008)

A Crossing of Zebras: Animal Packs in Poetry (Maddox, 2008)

Sugar Cane: A Caribbean Rapunzel (Storace, 2007)

One Million Things: A Visual Encyclopedia (Bryan, 2008)

Find more arts activities under these featured social studies books (Chapter 3):

Warriors: All the Truth, Tactics, and Triumphs of History's Greatest Fighters (Harpur, 2007)

The Brothers' War: Civil War Voices in Verse (Lewis, 2007)

The Many Rides of Paul Revere (Giblin, 2007)

Dear Mr. Rosenwald (Weatherford, 2006)

Muhammad (Demi, 2003)

Seven Miles to Freedom: The Robert Smalls Story (Halfmann, 2008)

Ain't Nothing but a Man: My Quest to Find the Real John Henry (Nelson & Aronson, 2008)

Lady Liberty: A Biography (Rappaport, 2008)

Find more arts activities under these featured math books (Chapter 4):

Twenty-One Elephants and Still Standing (Prince, 2005)

Wild Fibonacci: Nature's Secret Code Revealed (Hulme, 2005)

Skyscraper (Curlee, 2007)

Knights and Armor (Firth, 2006)

The Great Number Rumble: A Story of Math in Surprising Places (Lee & O'Reilly, 2007)

The World Record Paper Airplane Book (Blackburn & Lammers, 2006)

Go Figure! A Totally Cool Book about Numbers (Ball, 2005)

Show Me the Money: How to Make Cents of Economics (Hall, 2008)

A Very Improbable Story (Einhorn, 2008)

Find more arts activities under these featured science books (Chapter 5):

Solving Crimes with Trace Evidence (Jeffrey, 2008)

Team Moon: How 400,000 People Landed Apollo 11 on the Moon (Thimmesh, 2006)

The Leaping, Sliding, Sprinting, Riding Science Book: 50 Super Sports Science Activities (Mercer, 2006)

The Down-to-Earth Guide to Global Warming (David & Gordon, 2007)

Amazing Leonardo da Vinci Inventions You Can Build Yourself (Anderson, 2006)

Ouch! How Your Body Makes It through a Very Bad Day (Walker, 2007)

Cool Stuff 2.0 and How It Works (Woodford & Woodcock, 2007)

The Story of Salt (Kurlansky, 2006)

Into the Volcano: A Volcano Researcher at Work (Donovan-O'Meara, 2005)

Appendix A

Web Resources

Authors and illustrators on the Web
http://www.ucalgary.ca/~dkbrown/authors.html

Book Links **Web Connections**
http://www.ala.org/ala/aboutala/offices/publishing/booklinks/index.cfm

Caldecott Medal home page
http://www.ala.org/ala/mgrps/divs/alsc/awardsgrants/bookmedia/caldecottmedal/caldecottmedal.cfm

Children's Book Council—Children's Choices books lists
http://www.cbcbooks.org/

The Horn Book—Horn Book Awards
http://www.hbook.com/bghb/default.asp

International Reading Association
http://www.reading.org

> **IRA Children's and Young Adult's Book Awards**
> http://www.reading.org/association/awards/childrens_ira.html

National Council for the Social Studies
http://www.ncss.org

> **Curriculum standards for social studies**
> http://www.ncss.org/standards/strands

National Council of Teachers of English
http://www.ncte.org

> **Orbis Pictus Award [nonfiction]**
> http://www.ncte.org/awards/orbispictus

National Council of Teachers of Mathematics
http://www.nctm.org

> **Principles & Standards for School Mathematics**
> http://standards.nctm.org/document/appendix/numb.htm

National Education Technology Standards—Curriculum and Content Area Standards, Science
http://cnets.iste.org/currstands/cstands-s58.html

National Science Teachers Association
http://www.nsta.org

> **Outstanding Science Trade Books for Children**
> http://www.nsta.org/ostbc

National Standards for Arts Education
http://artsedge.kennedy-center.org/teach/standards.cfm

Pacific Northwest Library Association—Young Readers Choice Awards
http://www.pnla.org/yrca/index.htm

PBS Teachers book links
http://www.pbs.org/teachers/bookslinks

ReadWriteThink
http://www.readwritethink.org

Robert F. Sibert Informational Book Medal
http://www.ala.org/ala/alsc/awardsscholarships/literaryawds/sibertmedal/Sibert_Medal.htm

ThinkFinity
http://www.thinkfinity.org

Appendix B

Suggested Teaching Strategies

Anticipation guide: This guide helps activate students' background knowledge, stimulates interest in the text, and provides a purpose for reading. The teacher creates a list of statements that students read before reading the text, marking whether they agree or disagree. To develop the statements, identify several major topics in the reading, keeping in mind what students might already know. Develop four to six statements (using true/false, yes/no, or agree/disagree) that are general enough to stimulate discussion and might help clarify misconceptions about the topic. Students can answer in small groups or individually. Answers are shared, along with justifications for their choices. Students read the text and then review the statements and decide if they would change their answer and why. Every answer does not need to be in the reading, thus encouraging further research on the topic.

Before reading: (Circle one)		**Topic:** The moon	**After reading:** (Circle one)	
Agree	Disagree	During a lunar eclipse, the moon goes behind the sun.	Agree	Disagree
Agree	Disagree	A lunar cycle lasts about 30 days.	Agree	Disagree
Agree	Disagree	The phrase "once in a blue moon" comes from when we see a full moon twice in the same month.	Agree	Disagree

An example of an anticipation guide.

For more information and a blank template see http://www.greece.k12.ny.us/instruction/ela/6-12/Reading/Reading%20Strategies/anticipation%20guide.htm.

Bio poem: Students follow a set of prompts to write poems about biographical subjects. They must research (or read a biography) about the subject in order to create the nine-line poem. Line 1: First name of subject; Line 2: Four adjectives/phrases to describe the subject; Line 3: Husband/wife/child of _____; Line 4: Lover of (three things or people); Line 5: Who feels (three emotions); Line 6: Who fears (three things); Line 7: Who would like to (three things); Line 8: Resident of (city/state/country); Line 9: Last name of subject (Hancock, 2007).

Cause and effect: These organizers are created to demonstrate understanding about the effects of particular events. Students (or teachers) list events and the resulting response.

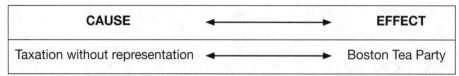

CAUSE	⟵⟶	EFFECT
Taxation without representation	⟵⟶	Boston Tea Party

An example of a cause-and-effect organizer.

See http://www.literacymatters.org/content/text/cause.htm for additional information and templates.

Character trading cards: This strategy is useful with fiction or nonfiction. Students use what they know about a person in the book to provide information about his or her description, development of action/events, and the students' impression of the character. Space is provided to create a drawing of the person described. Use the ReadWriteThink.org site for a quick and easy way to create character cards: http://www.readwritethink.org/materials/trading_cards/.

Jigsaw: Students are divided into small groups of about four or five. Each group member is assigned a topic to research or study. In every group, there should be members assigned to the same topics. Students then leave their home teams to join an expert group made up of students who were assigned the same topic. After expert groups discuss the topic in detail, students return to their home teams and act as discussion leaders on their topics (Parker & Jarolimek, 1997).

Kamishibai storytelling cards: A fictional story is broken down into 10 to 15 sequential sections. Students create an illustrated "story card" for each section. They also summarize the text, which is adhered to the back of the cards, with the summary for the first story card on the back of the LAST story card. The summary for story card 2 is adhered to the back of story card 1, and so on.

Literature circles: This format for discussion assigns roles to each student. The student reads, responds, and brings to the discussion particular information based on his or her role. Typical roles are discussion leader, historian, director of visual arts, and etymologist. For complete information, see Kelley and Clausen-Grace (2007).

Matrix: This graphic organizer is a way for students to compare key attributes and characteristics of items (people, places, events, etc.). Using a chart, such as the following one, column and row headings label important characteristics and/or qualities to be compared.

	Characteristic 1	Characteristic 2	Characteristic 3	Characteristic 4
Quality 1				
Quality 2				
Quality 3				

An example of a matrix.

Papermaking: A number of websites provide easy instructions for students to make paper. Try:

> http://www.tutorials.com/06/0697/0697.asp

> http://www.historyforkids.org/crafts/china/paper.htm

> http://www.kidsgardening.com/paper-pg2.html

The basic materials needed are scrap paper, water, screening, and a large tub of water. It is an excellent way to recycle paper.

Readers' theater: Students create scripts following the reading of a text. Scripts can be created from fiction, nonfiction, and poetry. Essential information is selected for the speaking parts. Students can be encouraged to use new vocabulary learned from the text. Multiple readings of the script encourage fluency. (For ideas and Web links, see http://www.aaronshep.com/rt/RTE.html.)

Role-play: A role-play involves considering a situation from another person's viewpoint. A role-play scenario must have character/s, a problem, and a setting. Example: Two students see a friend shoplifting at the drugstore. What should they do? Discuss the results (Cornett, 1999).

Salt crystals: Crystals are grown by dissolving salt in boiling water. There are numerous websites that provide detailed directions. One of these is http://chemistry.about.com/od/growingcrystals/ht/saltcrystals.htm.

Salt dough: Items can be created from salt dough. Mix 1½ cups of flour, 1½ cups of salt, and 1⅛ cups of water, stirring slowly until you get the consistency of bread dough. Shape immediately into desired configuration. Allow forty-eight hours drying time. The finished product may be painted if desired (Thomas & Pagel, 1998).

Shape poems: Words to a poem are arranged to create the shape of the object being described. For example, a poem about a snake may be words arranged in a curvy line that create the shape of a snake's body. If the poem were about rain, the words could be arranged to look like rain falling.

Story theater: One or more narrators read dialogue and narrative aloud, while other students interpret the action and feelings through pantomime. A story in which action is essential to the plot makes a good choice (Pappas, Kiefer, & Levstik, 1995).

Venn diagram: John Venn created the Venn diagram in 1881. He was a mathematician who wanted to show the inclusive and exclusive relationship between two or three subsets. Overlapping circles are drawn. The outer parts of the circle contain information that is exclusive to the topic of the circle. The overlapping section contains information that is inclusive to both (or all) the circles. Use the Read-WriteThink.org site for a quick and easy way to create a Venn diagram (http://www.readwritethink.org/materials/venn/). See further ideas for two-circle and three-circle Venn diagrams at http://www.readwritethink.org/student_mat/student_material.asp?id=6.

References

Baghban, M. (2007). Immigration in childhood: Using picture books to cope. *The Social Studies, 98*(2), 71–76.

Baker, J. (1987). *Where the forest meets the sea.* New York: Greenwillow.

Baker, J. (1991). *Window.* New York: Puffin.

Beane, J. A. (1993). *A middle school curriculum: From rhetoric to reality* (2nd ed.). Columbus, OH: National Middle School Association.

Bishop, R. S., & Hickman, J. (1992). Four or fourteen or forty: Picture books are for everyone. In S. Benedict, & L. Carlisle (Eds.), *Beyond words: Picture books for older readers and writers* (pp. 1–10). Portsmouth, NH: Heinemann.

Brozo, W. G., & Flynt, E. (2007). Content literacy: Fundamental toolkit elements. *The Reading Teacher, 61*(2), 192–194.

Brozo, W. G., & Simpson, M. L. (2007). *Content literacy for today's adolescents: Honoring diversity and building competence.* Upper Saddle River, NJ: Merrill Prentice Hall.

Bunting, E. (1996). *Going home.* Illustrated by David Diaz. New York: HarperCollins.

Bunting, E. (1994). *Smoky night.* Illustrated by David Diaz. San Diego: Harcourt Brace.

Burress, C. (February 28, 2006). Groups seeking textbook revisions: Lessons on life in ancient India stir education hearing. *San Francisco Chronicle.* Retrieved February 6, 2009, from http://www.sfgate.com/cgi-bin/article.cgi?f=/c/a/2006/02/28/BAGM5HFU5I1.DTL.

Camp, D. (2000). It takes two: Teaching with Twin Texts of fact and fiction. *The Reading Teacher, 53*(5), 400–408.

Carlisle, L. R. (1992). Picture books: An easy place to think. In S. Benedict, & L. Carlisle (Eds.), *Beyond words: Picture books for older readers and writers* (pp. 49–58). Portsmouth, NH: Heinemann.

Chambliss, M. J., & Calfee, R. C. (1998). *Textbooks for learning: Nurturing children's minds.* Malden, MA: Blackwell Publishers.

Chick, K. A. (2006). Fostering student collaboration through the use of historical picture books. *The Social Studies, 97*(4), 152–157.

Connor, J. J. (2003). "The textbooks never said anything about . . ." Adolescents respond to *The Middle Passage: White Ships/Black Cargo. Journal of Adolescent & Adult Literacy, 47*(3), 240–246.

Cornett, C. E. (1999). *The arts as meaning makers: Integrating literature and the arts throughout the curriculum.* Upper Saddle River, NJ: Merrill.

Costello, B., & Kolodziej, N. J. (2006). A middle school teacher's guide for selecting picture books. *Middle School Journal, 38*(1), 27–33.

Daniels, H., & Zemelman, S. (2003/2004). New needs, new curriculum—out with textbooks, in with learning. *Educational Leadership: Journal of the Department of Supervision and Curriculum Development, NEA, 61*(4), 36–40.

Daniels, H., & Zemelman, S. (2004). *Subjects matter: Every teacher's guide to content-area reading.* Portsmouth, NH: Heinemann.

David, L., & Gordon, C. (2007). *The down-to-earth guide to global warming.* New York: Scholastic. (NF)

Einhorn, E. (2008). *A very improbable story.* Illustrated by Adam Gustavson. Watertown, MA: Charlesbridge.

Farris, P. J., & Fuhler, C. J. (1994). Developing social studies concepts through picture books. *The Reading Teacher, 47*(5), 380–387.

Fingerson, J., & Killeen, E. B. (2006). Picture books for young adults: How to inspire, connect, and reach early teens with a familiar format—picture books. *Teacher Librarian, 33*(4), 32–34.

Fisher, D., & Frey, N. (2008). *Improving adolescent literacy: Content area strategies at work.* Upper Saddle River, NJ: Pearson/Merrill/Prentice Hall.

Freeman, E. B., & Person, D. G. (1998). *Connecting informational children's books with content area learning.* Boston, MA: Allyn & Bacon.

Giorgis, C., & Hartman, K. J. (2000). Using picture books to support middle school curricula. *Middle School Journal, 31*(4), 34–41.

Hancock, M. R. (2007). *Language arts: Extending the possibilities.* Upper Saddle River, NJ: Pearson/Merrill/Prentice Hall.

Harpur, J. (2007). *Warriors: All the truth, tactics, and triumphs of history's greatest fighters.* New York: Atheneum Books for Young Readers.

Harris, T. L., & Hodges, R. E. (Eds.). (1995). *The literacy dictionary: The vocabulary of reading and writing.* Newark, DE: International Reading Association.

Hibbing, A. N., & Rankin-Erickson, J. L. (2003). A picture is worth a thousand words: Using visual images to improve comprehension for middle school struggling readers. *The Reading Teacher, 56*(8), 758–770.

Hickman, P., Pollard-Durodola, S., & Vaughn, S. (May 2004). Storybook reading: Improving vocabulary and comprehension for English-language learners. *The Reading Teacher, 57*(8), 720–730.

Hubisz, J. (2003). Middle-school texts don't make the grade. *Physics Today, 56*(5), 50–54.

Ivey, G. (2003). The intermediate grades—"The teacher makes it more explainable" and other reasons to read aloud in the intermediate grades. *The Reading Teacher, 56*(8), 812–814.

Johnson, H., & Freedman, L. (2004). *Content area literature circles: Using discussion for learning across the curriculum.* Norwood, MA: Christopher-Gordon.

Johnson, N. J., & Giorgis, C. (2001). Children's books: Interacting with the curriculum. *The Reading Teacher, 55*(2), 204–213.

Kelley, M. J., & Clausen-Grace, N. (2007). *Comprehension shouldn't be silent: From strategy instruction to student independence.* Newark, DE: International Reading Association.

Kettel, R. P., & Douglas, N. L. (2003). Comprehending multiple texts: A theme approach incorporating the best of children's literature. *Voices from the Middle, 11*(1), 43–49.

Klingel, C. F. (2008). *You let the cat out of the bag! (and other crazy animal sayings).* Illustrated by Mernie Gallagher-Cole. Mankato, MN: Child's World.

Krull, K. (1996). *Wilma unlimited: How Wilma Rudolph became the world's fastest woman.* Illustrated by David Diaz. San Diego: Harcourt Brace.

Lamping, S., Mack, N., & Johnson, A. B. (2007). Prompting engagement: Young adult literature, picture books and traditional themes for secondary students. *Ohio Journal of English Language Arts, 47*(2), 38–47.

Landt, S. M. (2007). Using picture books to arouse interest in the study of geographic areas. *The Social Studies, 98*(1), 9–12.

Lee, C., Gray, V., & O'Reilly, G. (2007). *The great number rumble: The story of math in surprising places.* Toronto, ON: Annick Press.

Luke, J. L., & Myers, C. M. (1995). Toward peace: Using literature to aid conflict resolution. *Childhood Education, 71*(2), 66–69.

Manifold, M. C. (2007). The healing picture book: An aesthetic of sorrow. *Teacher Librarian, 34*(3), 20–26.

Manning, M. L., & Bucher, K. T. (2009). *Teaching in the middle school* (3rd ed.). Boston: Allyn & Bacon.

Manning, M. L., & Baruth, L. G. (2004). *Multicultural education of children and adolescents.* Boston: Allyn & Bacon.

Marcus, L. S. (2002). *Ways of telling: Conversations on the art of the picture book.* New York: Dutton Children's Books.

Mercer, B. (2006). *The leaping, sliding, sprinting, riding science book: 50 super sports science activities.* Illustrated by Tom LaBaff. New York: Lark Books.

Moore, D. W., Bean, T., Birdyshaw, D., & Tycik, J. (1999). *Adolescent literacy: A position statement.* Newark, DE: International Reading Association.

National Council of Teachers of English. (1996). *Standards for the English Language Arts.* Urbana, IL: NCTE and IRA.

National Council of Teachers of English. (May 2004). *A call to action: What we know about adolescent literacy and ways to support teachers in meeting students' needs.* Urbana, IL: National Council of Teachers of English. Retrieved from http://www.ncte.org/standards.

National Council of Teachers of English. (2007). *Adolescent literacy: An NCTE policy research brief.* Urbana, IL: National Council of Teachers of English. Retrieved from http://www.ncte.org/library/NCTEFiles/Resources/PolicyResearch/AdolLitResearchBrief.pdf.

Olness, R. (2007). *Using literature to enhance content area instruction: A guide for*

K-5 teachers. Newark, DE: International Reading Association.

Pantaleo, S. (2007). "How could that be?": Reading Banyai's *Zoom* and *Re-zoom*. *Language Arts, 84*(3), 222–233.

Pappas, C. C., Kiefer, B. Z., & Levstik, L. S. (1995). *An integrated language perspective in the elementary school: Theory into action*. White Plains, NY: Longman.

Parker, W. C., & Jarolimek, J. (1997). *Social studies in elementary education*. Upper Saddle River, NJ: Merrill.

Rappaport, D. (2008). *Lady Liberty: A biography*. Illustrated by Matt Tavares. Cambridge, MA: Candlewick Press.

Ravitch, D. (2003). *The language police: How pressure groups restrict what students learn*. New York: Knopf.

Reid, S. E. (2002). *Book bridges for ESL students: Using young adult and children's literature to teach ESL*. Lanham, MD: Scarecrow Press.

ReadWriteThink.org. (2008). Retrieved from http://www.readwritethink.org/standards/index.html.

Richardson, J. S., Morgan, R. F., & Fleener, C. E. (2006). *Reading to learn in the content areas* (6th ed.). Belmont, CA: Thomson/Wadsworth.

Sadler, C. R. (2001). *Comprehension strategies for middle grade learners: A handbook for content area teachers*. Newark, DE: International Reading Association.

Sanacore, J. (1993). Supporting a literature-based approach across the curriculum. *Journal of Reading, 37*(3), 240–244.

Saunders, S. L. (1999). *Look—and learn!: Using picture books in grades five through eight*. Portsmouth, NH: Heinemann.

Sheridan, N. (2001, Fall). Using picture books in content area classes: Some applications for content area reading. *ACEI Focus on Elementary, 14*(1), 1–6.

Silverman, L. (2007). Focus on the Holocaust: Bearing witness through picture books. *School Library Journal, 53*(3), 62–66.

Thomas, J. E., & Pagel, D. (1998). *The ultimate book of kid concoctions: More than 65 wacky, wild & crazy concoctions*. Strongsville, OH: Kid Concoctions Company.

Tunnell, M. O., & Jacobs, J. S. (2008). *Children's literature briefly* (4th ed.). Upper Saddle River, NJ: Pearson/Merrill/Prentice Hall.

Vacca, R. T., & Vacca, J. A. L. (2008). *Content area reading: Literacy and learning across the curriculum* (9th ed.). Boston: Pearson/Allyn & Bacon.

Wolfenbarger, C. D., & Sipe, L. R. (2007). A unique visual and literary art form: Recent research on picturebooks. *Language Arts, 84*(3), 273–280.

Wysocki, B. (2004). A thousand words: The picture-perfect link to the curriculum. *School Library Journal, 50*(4), 8–12.

Zemelman, S., Daniels, H., & Hyde, A. A. (2005). *Best practice: Today's standards for teaching and learning in America's schools* (3rd ed.). Portsmouth, NH: Heinemann.

Authors

Mary Jo Fresch, a professor in the School of Teaching and Learning at The Ohio State University at Marion, holds a BS and an MS from the University of Akron and a PhD from The Ohio State University. Her teaching experiences include third grade, and literacy and children's literature courses at University of Akron, University of Nebraska (Lincoln), and in Melbourne, Australia, at The Royal Melbourne Institute and Deakin University. She presents nationally and internationally. Her articles appear in *Language Arts, Journal of Literacy Research, The Reading Teacher, Reading and Writing Quarterly,* and *Reading Psychology.* She coauthored *Teaching and Assessing Spelling, The Spelling List and Word Study Resource Book* (both Scholastic), and *Spelling for Writers* (Great Source). She edited *An Essential History of Current Reading Practices* (International Reading Association).

Mary Jo and her husband, Hank, enjoy travel and golf. They have two married children—Angela (and Nate) and Michael (and Lori).

Peggy Harkins has been teaching on The Ohio State University's regional campus at Marion, Ohio, since 1995. Currently, she balances her time between administrative work and teaching. She also has previous teaching experience at the third-grade level in Ohio and Pennsylvania. Her educational background includes a BS in elementary education from the University of Dayton, an MA in early and middle childhood education from The Ohio State University, and a PhD in developmental curriculum from The Ohio State University. She has presented at state and international conferences, and her research articles have appeared in *Childhood Education, Early Childhood Education Journal, The Reading Teacher, Young Children,* state journals, and special interest publications.

Peggy and her husband, Rich, share their home with hundreds of books (some of them picture books). They have two married sons and two preschool grandsons who benefit from their grandmother's love of great children's literature!

This book was typeset in Palatino and Helvetica by Barbara Frazier.
Typefaces used on the cover were Bembo and Helvetica Neue.
The book was printed on 50-lb. Williamsburg Offset paper by Versa Press, Inc.